THE CADOGAN ESTATE

QUI·INVIDET·MINOR·EST

THE CADOGAN ESTATE

The History of a Landed Family

ROBERT PEARMAN

Haggerston Press

LONDON

First published 1986
by the Haggerston Press
38 Kensington Place, London W8 7PR

Typeset by Inforum Ltd, Portsmouth
Printed in Great Britain
by Redwood Burn Ltd, Trowbridge

1 869812 01 8

For Lord Cadogan

Contents

Contents

Out of Monuments, Names, Wordes, Proverbs, Traditions, Private Recordes and Evidences, Fragments of Stories, Passages of Bookes, and the Like, We Doe Save and Recover Somewhat from the Deluge of Time

Lord Bacon *On The Advancement of Learning* Book II

Foreword

It became apparent to me while engaged upon some town planning research for the University of Reading that the Cadogan story was worth the telling, and with an earlier exhortation from Lord Cadogan in mind that he would like to see a formal family history in print, I have duly written this volume.

Virtually all the Cadogan family archives were lost in a fire during their removal from Chelsea House to Culford Hall in the early 1890s and hence the task has been one of knitting together many fragments of information from divers sources to form, hopefully, an intelligible whole.

I have been greatly assisted in my researches by the unstinting help given to me by the staff of many record offices and libraries including more particularly the local studies section of the Chelsea Library and the House of Lords Record Office. A little further from home much laudable patience was shown in the face of my myriad inquiries by, among others, Miss Catherine Fahy of the National Library of Ireland, Mr Phil Connolly of the Public Record Office in Ireland, Mr D.E. Williams of The National Library of Wales and Mr A.J. Parkinson of the Royal Commission on Ancient and Historic Monuments in Wales. The Dutch authorities were also extremely helpful. I thank them all and I also thank my wife Penny and my daughter Catherine for bearing with me during the period of gestation.

Votes of thanks are also due to Lord Stockton for his kind

permission to use an extract from his autobiography *Wind of Change*, to my literary mentor Mr William Lowndes of Bath for allowing me access to his personal library, to Miss Pam Molloy and to my former 'chief' Mr Dennis Bedingham of the Cadogan Office for their encouragement and assistance, and lastly and more importantly to Lord Cadogan for allowing a chartered surveyor the opportunity to indulge himself in the temporary role of historian and author.

Any mistakes in the book, and I fear that there may be some, are mine alone.

LONDON
March 1986

Robert Pearman

CHAPTER I

The Estate Today – A General Description

The Cadogan Estate in Chelsea is administered by companies on behalf of the Cadogan family whose titular head is the 7th Earl Cadogan. Dating from the mid-eighteenth century, it is one of the few remaining aristocratic estates in London and it ranks alongside, in terms of quality if not quantity, the Duke of Westminster's Grosvenor Estate and the estates of Lord Portman and Lord Howard de Walden.

The Estate which has its origins in the richly historic Manor of Chelsea, owned at different times by Westminster Abbey and by Henry VIII, covers in a fragmented manner some ninety-four acres of one of the capital's most fashionable residential districts. It stretches on a north/south axis from Knightsbridge to Cheyne Walk overlooking the River Thames and from Beaufort Street in the west to Cadogan Place in the east. It comprises, essentially, some 4000 flats, 700 houses, 300 shops and stores and 300,000 square feet of office space. The shops and stores include such well-known names as Laura Ashley, Boots, Jaeger, Peter Jones, W.H. Smith and last but by no means least, the General Trading Company which lies at the very heart of 'Sloane Ranger' territory.

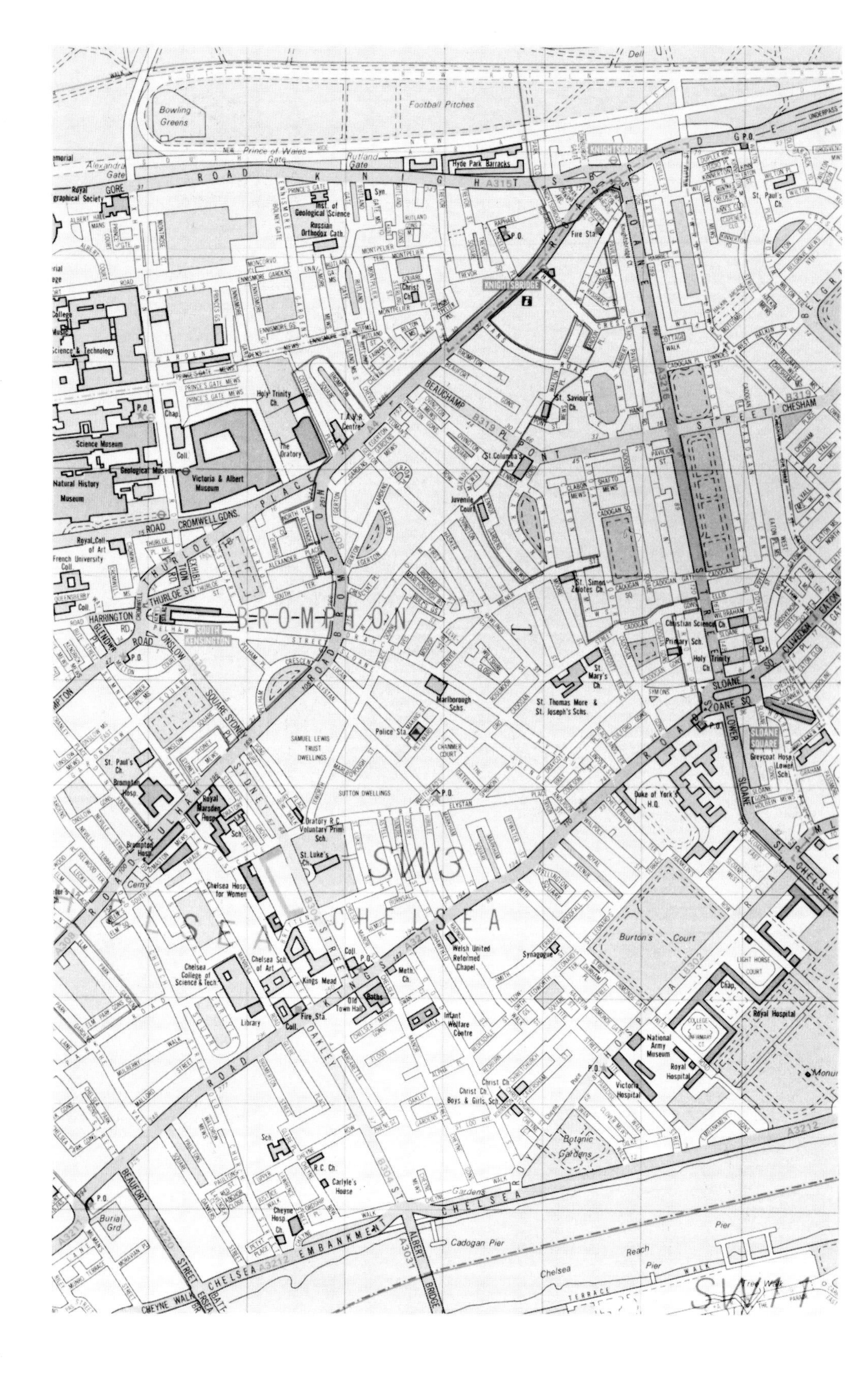

Football Pitches
Bowling Greens
Prince of Wales Gate
Rutland Gate
Alexandra Gate
Hyde Park Barracks
KNIGHTSBRIDGE
Royal Geographical Society
Inst. of Geological Science
Russian Orthodox Cath.
Syn.
Christ Ch.
Fire Sta.
Science & Technology
Holy Trinity Ch.
T.A.V.R. Centre
The Oratory
Science Museum
Geological Museum
Victoria & Albert Museum
Natural History Museum
CROMWELL GDNS.
Royal Coll. of Art
French University Coll.
BROMPTON
SOUTH KENSINGTON
St. Saviour's Ch.
St. Columba's Ch.
Juvenile Court
CHESHAM
St. Simon Zelotes Ch.
Christian Science Ch.
Primary Sch.
Holy Trinity Ch.
St. Mary's Ch.
St. Thomas More & St. Joseph's Schs.
Marlborough Schs.
Police Sta.
SAMUEL LEWIS TRUST DWELLINGS
SUTTON DWELLINGS
SLOANE SQUARE
Greycoat Hosp. Lower Sch.
Duke of York's H.Q.
St. Paul's Ch.
Brompton Hosp.
Royal Marsden Hosp.
Oratory R.C. Voluntary Prim. Sch.
St. Luke's Ch.
SW3
CHELSEA
Chelsea Hosp. for Women
Burton's Court
Welsh United Reformed Chapel
Synagogue
Chelsea Sch. of Art
Chelsea College of Science & Tech.
Kings Mead
Meth. Ch.
Old Town Hall
Baths
Library
Fire Sta.
Infant Welfare Centre
LIGHT HORSE COURT
Chap.
Royal Hospital
National Army Museum
Victoria Hospital
Christ Ch.
Christ Ch. Boys & Girls Sch.
Botanic Gardens
Sch.
R.C. Ch.
Carlyle's House
Cheyne Hosp.
Burial Grd.
Cadogan Pier
Chelsea Reach
Pier
SW11
CHELSEA EMBANKMENT
ALBERT BRIDGE
CHEYNE WALK
BEAUFORT STREET
KING'S ROAD
FULHAM ROAD
SLOANE STREET

Chelsea (opposite page) and the Cadogan Estate today (above: hatched areas).

The Cadogan Hotel

The acreage has reduced substantially over the years due both to the vagaries of commercial necessity and to the generosity of the Cadogan family to local institutions. The 5th Earl Cadogan, for example, donated land for the construction of workmen's dwellings in 1890 and for the later building of the Chelsea Hospital for Women.

Visitors both from home and abroad, not unnaturally, find this central area of the capital with its fine blend of old and modern buildings attractive, with the result that there

Cadogan Place – South garden

are a number of very luxurious hotels situated on the Estate including the dominating Hyatt Carlton Tower, the Chelsea Hotel, the Royal Court Hotel and the Cadogan Hotel where, in 1895, Oscar Wilde was arrested prior to his imprisonment in Reading Gaol. There is also the very comfortable Sloane Club in Lower Sloane Street which moved to its present location in 1947.

Perhaps the most famous building architecturally on the Estate is the Danish Embassy in Sloane Street, designed by the Danish architect Arne Jacobsen. There are other interesting examples of work elsewhere by Walter Gropius, Henry Holland and R. Norman Shaw.[1]

One of the more attractive aspects of the Estate, especially in spring time, is its private gardens which cover one sixth of the total area. The garden at Cadogan Place has the reputation of being the largest private garden in London and covers seven-and-a-half acres of tree-lined walks, lawns, flower beds, tennis courts and a children's play area with swings and a very popular sandpit. There are two fine bronze statues by David Wynne, 'The Dancers' in the north garden and the 'Girl with the Doves' in the south garden. Opposite this statue is a sun dial erected in memory of Christopher Head, a former honorary secretary of the Gardens who perished when the *Titanic* foundered in 1912.

There are twelve private gardens in all and second in terms of size to Cadogan Place is the garden serving the massively impressive Victorian red-brick Cadogan Square properties. This covers two acres and also has tennis courts, with a resident professional to coach those with or without Wimbledon aspirations. H.G. Wells played tennis here in 1928 at the invitation of Arnold Bennett, then a resident of Cadogan Square.[2] Other gardens include Hans Place – the oldest and where perhaps once Jane Austen[3] sought literary inspiration – Chelsea Square, Tedworth Square, Sloane Gardens and Lower Sloane Street. The decapitated granite monument inset at the southern periphery of the Hans Place garden is in memory of Major-General Sir Herbert Stewart, a one-time resident in the late nineteenth century who was involved in the construction of Herbert Crescent which bears his name.

At the northern end of Cadogan Square lies the very picturesque Shafto Mews with its red-brick arched entrance and cobbled roadway. At the time of their construction during the reign of Queen Victoria mews properties locally were intended for the accommodation of carriage horses with rooms above the stables for grooms and other servants from the nearby mansion houses. Unfortunately, few

Cadogan Square – North-west side

Pavilion Road – Old mews house

examples of the original mews houses remain, most having been in recent years either rebuilt or converted into bijou town residences, but there are still a few examples to be seen in Clabon Mews, to the rear of the western terrace of Cadogan Square and in the northern part of Pavilion Road behind Hans Place.

There are a good number of churches serving the spiritual needs of the Estate's residents including St Luke's, the Chelsea parish church in Sydney Street with its open early Gothic aspect, high tower and lofty nave where Charles Dickens married in 1836, and the brick-and-stone-fronted and perhaps less inspiring Holy Trinity just off Sloane Square. Apart from its underground station, Sloane Square

General Trading Company in Sloane Street

houses the Royal Court Theatre associated with George Bernard Shaw and John Osborne and many eminent actors including Dame Peggy Ashcroft, Sir Alec Guinness and Rex Harrison.

Sloane Square brings together the two main thoroughfares both serving and bisecting the Estate: Sloane Street, running virtually north to south, and Kings Road lying approximately east to west. Towards the Sloane Square end of Sloane Street are to be found the General Trading Company with its very welcoming restaurant and the newly extended supermarket premises of Partridges in which it is a delight to shop. Progressing then northwards towards Pont Street and Knightsbridge there is on the west side a mix of Victorian and Georgian houses, now generally converted into apartments, and twentieth-century blocks of flats including Cadogan House and Grosvenor Court.

Southern end of Sloane Street showing Partridges and Liscartan House

On the opposite side of the road just past Ellis Street lie the gardens fronting the stuccoed houses of Cadogan Place which may only be glimpsed when the trees are in leaf. Passing the Cadogan Hotel, crossing over Pont Street and continuing northwards one then arrives at the very modern Danish Embassy and, two doors further along, the Peruvian Embassy housed in a red-brick Victorian building. This is diametrically opposite the Hyatt Carlton Tower hotel, shop and office complex in which one of the tenants is a branch of Coutts Bank, established in 1692. Messrs Coutts held some of the very early Sloane family bank accounts.

From here until Knightsbridge itself, if one leaves aside the Chelsea Hotel, the shops are the important feature, more especially those dealing in high fashion for ladies. There is also a branch of Laura Ashley, a showroom for Aston Martin and, virtually at the northern extremity of the Estate, the Truslove and Hanson bookshop with 40,000 volumes to delight the most demanding bibliophile. It may be noted in passing that the land upon which Harvey Nichols stands at one time formed part of the Estate.

If Sloane Street might be accused of being a little straight-laced such an accusation could not be levelled at Kings Road which became legendary in the Swinging Sixties and today is the chief place of pilgrimage for the rainbow-hued 'punk' element of the population. Not surprisingly, the many clothes' shops and boutiques, some with their pulsating rock music spilling out onto the pavement, are oriented towards fashion for the young and the young at heart. Jaeger have a shop here as well as another in Sloane Street and there is one of the very good John Lewis Waitrose supermarkets. John Lewis is also represented by the Peter

Northern end of Sloane Street with the Chelsea Hotel in mid-distance

Kings Road looking towards Sloane Square

Jones department store which is dear to the hearts of all Chelsea residents.

The Kings Road was at one time just that, dating back to the days of King Charles II (1660–1685), and it was not opened to the public until 1830. It gives access to the western area of the Estate which, with many streets of Victorian terraced houses, in the main is not so architecturally interesting as the eastern area. One of the exceptions is Cheyne Walk where the Georgian and later period houses overlooking the river are outstanding. Also located in the western area is Flood Street, until recently home of Mrs Margaret Thatcher, and Royal Hospital Road where the Chelsea Physic Garden lies, whose trustees pay to the Estate a perpetual rent of £5 per annum for their three-and-a-quarter-acre site. The garden was founded in 1673 and in 1722 Sir Hans Sloane, who had earlier purchased the Manor of Chelsea, conveyed a virtual freehold interest in the land to the then tenants, the Society of Apothecaries. It was the marriage of one of Sir Hans's daughters to the 1st Earl Cadogan's brother that gave rise to the Cadogan Chelsea Estate in 1753. The garden, which produces specialist herbs and flowers, was opened to the public in 1983.

One recent innovation by the Estate is to make it a requirement in all new leases that the external brickwork and stonework to buildings be cleaned and restored on a regular basis. This has already made a tremendous difference to the visual aspect and the full impact may be seen in Sloane Gardens, where all but one or two of the old Victorian leases have recently been renewed including those of the four houses comprising the excellent Garden House School whose girls during the colder times of the

Flood Street

Ormonde Gate

Herbert Crescent

year are to be seen in their serried turquoise ranks.

The Estate has other well known schools within its boundaries including Sussex House in Cadogan Square and Hill House School in Hans Place where the Prince of Wales was once a pupil. The Princess of Wales who before her marriage was a kindergarten teacher, was also a regular visitor to the Estate when she took her young charges for dancing lessons at the nearby academy of Miss Violet Ballantine then situated at 12 Herbert Crescent. Miss Ballantine who taught the daughters of local residents for over thirty years only retired in 1983 and, sad to relate, died two years later.[4]

Another pupil of a former school at 22 Hans Place was Caroline Ponsonby at the end of the eighteenth century who later, as Lady Caroline Lamb, became famous as the thwarted mistress of Lord Byron. The present building on the site, erected in 1883, is used as commercial offices.

A walk around the Estate will indicate to the discerning eye a firm management policy and this is administered by a small staff operating from the Estate Office in Cadogan Square. They are assisted in legal matters by the firm of Lee & Pembertons who occupy premises close-by in Pont Street and who, through the Lee and Pemberton families, have acted for the Estate for many years. A Private Act of Parliament which the Estate obtained in 1825 was prepared by Mr R.E.N. Lee.

CHAPTER II

Welsh Origins

The Cadogan family is descended in male line from Cuhelyn, Prince of Fferlys and his son Elstan Glodrydd, a chieftain of Radnorshire who founded the fifth of the Royal Tribes of Wales. Little is known on any good authority of either father or son apart from the fact that they both lived at or about the turn of the millennium. Given the social structures of the time they would certainly have been fighting men, a supposition which is supported by a translation of the Celtic 'Cadogan' into 'Battle-Keenness'.

Elstan Glodrydd had one son Cadwgan (the family name was Anglicised in the fifteenth century although the pronunciation is essentially the same) who was rather more prolific with three sons called Idnerth of Malienydd, Goronwy and Llewelyn. Cadwgan was used as a baptismal name until the late eighteenth century.

From Llewelyn, who was slain in 1099 in a border feud, springs the present family line and until 1548 one can only speculate as to how these particular Cadogans lived.

It seems reasonably certain from the available evidence that Llewelyn's descendants would have closely allied themselves to the general cause of the Cadogan family as a whole, namely the protection of the family lands both from the Norman invaders and, later, the Marcher Barons.

Idnerth had one son Madog who, before his death in 1140, appears to have been a very active warrior and indeed a very active father, siring five sons. The eldest two, Hywel and Cadwgan, both died in battle in 1142. The third son Marredud fared little better and he was killed by a Marcher Lord, one Hugh Mortimer, in 1146. By what transpired later the Mortimers were clearly the Cadogans' deadly foes. Madog's remaining sons, great-nephews of Llewelyn, were longer lived. Cadwallon ruled as Prince of Maelienydd and Ceri while Einion Clud ruled as Prince of Elfael. Their lands which lay 'between the upper waters of the Wye and the Severn' are today located in the County of Powys, Maelienydd and Ceri to the north-east close to Llandrindod Wells with Elfael to the south-east in the Painscastle area.

As with most families all was not sweetness and light and in 1160, for some reason unknown, Cadwallon seized Einion Clud and made him over as a captive to the northern Prince Owain Gwynedd who promptly surrendered him into the custody of Henry II. Einion was imprisoned in Worcester Castle but, clearly being a man of some resolve, he later escaped. By 1164 Cadwallon and Einion had joined forces under the leadership of Owain, who by now appears not to have been on such good terms with his monarch, to gain an initial victory over Henry's English army.

By 1175 peace was restored and in June of that year Henry, having earlier returned to England, met with the Welsh princes at Gloucester with a view to cementing the new-found good relations. Cadwallon and Einion Clud took the opportunity to establish their claims to their traditional lands by promising to pay a consideration to the

Crown of 1000 cattle or £333 6s 8d. The cattle remained in their Welsh pastures and only £122 12s 0d was ever paid.

Cadwallon was to live but four more years and in 1179, two years after the death of his brother Einion Clud, he was killed by followers of Roger, heir to the Mortimer estates, as he was returning from the king's presence under the protection of a royal safe-conduct. As a result of the king's honour being impugned the matter was treated as more serious than a local feud and some of the offenders were put to death while Roger was cast into prison.

Cadwallon had two sons (daughters were presumably thought not worth recording), Maelgwn who died in 1197 and Hywel, while Einion Clud's union was similarly blessed with two sons called Einion o'r Porth who died in 1191 and the more prosaically named Walter. During a visit to Wales in 1187 by the Archbishop of Canterbury, who was intent upon raising a body of crusaders, it appears that among the 3000 well-armed men who donned the cross were Maelgwn and his cousin Einion, although whether they ever reached the Holy Land is unknown.

At some time prior to 1197, Cadwallon's sons were deprived of a substantial part of their patrimony in Ceri and Maelienydd when the Mortimers seized their castle at Cymaron. There had been an earlier exchange of this fortress with the opposing faction, and in that year the death of Maelgwn was a further blow to Welsh power in the district. The death of Einion o'r Porth had opened up the way for the invaders to take over the lands in Elfael so that by the end of the twelfth century the family's fortunes were very much on the wane.

A castle in the family is always rather exciting, so it may

be worthwhile digressing at this point to consider what sort of building this was. From what little remains of the site, some ten miles east of Llandrindod Wells on the edge of the Radnor Forest, the castle appears to have been an earthwork structure known as a 'motte and bailey' castle. The bailey comprised the main buildings, hall and living accommodation, protected by a rampart and ditch while the motte was a large pile of earth supporting a timber watch-tower.

Castle Cymaron was well positioned on naturally rising ground in an angle formed by a stream called the Cymaron and one of its tributaries. The entire position, save on the water side where the site was at its highest point, was surrounded by a moat. One can only speculate as to the appearance of the castle itself. No doubt the earthworks were cased by great timber walls, possibly crenellated, which might have been plastered and painted so as to look like stone giving an appearance more like the traditional stone-built castle. Castle Cymaron therefore probably presented a very brave sight in its heyday.

Save the bare note of the continuance of the line the Cadogans then drop from historical view until 1548 when Cadwgan ap William appears, living with his wife Catherine and three sons at a modest farmhouse further south in Trostry Fach in Monmouthshire. The 'ap' simply means 'son of' while Trostry Fach may be Anglicised as 'Lower Trostre' which on the contemporary map is two miles from Glascoed near to Pontypool in the County of Gwent.

The farmhouse in part-modernised form remains to this day. It is a rectangular, single storeyed building with a semi-attic under a part stone-tiled and part modern slate roof. White painted, its rendered stone walls are two feet six inches thick, patched here and there with brickwork and two buttresses support the west wall. The interior contains many sixteenth-century thick wooden ceiling beams with broad chamfers: altogether a house built to endure.

Cadwgan ap William had three grandsons: Cadwgan ap William Cadwgan who died in 1647, Henry Cadogan, and the youngest John Cadogan. (Lower Trostre in due time passed to the eldest son and so on eventually to his grandson Richard Cadogan who sold the property in 1670.) Henry, it may be reasonably suggested, needed a good dowry and this he appears to have achieved by marrying Catherine, daughter of Thomas Stradling of Glamorgan, nephew of Sir Thomas Stradling of St Donat's Castle also in Glamorgan. Henry and Catherine had only the one son, William Cadogan born at Cardiff on 5 February 1600 during the reign of Queen Elizabeth I, and it was he, with a reputation as a mercenary, who eventually went to Ireland in search of fame and fortune.

Lower Trostre Farmhouse today

CHAPTER III

Land in Ireland

It is likely that William Cadogan, gentleman, was educated at one of the grammar schools established in Wales after the Reformation, where the curriculum would have included the study of Greek and Latin in preparation for some useful later employment in the universities or the professions.

The patrimony comprised in Lower Trostre had by-passed William's father, Henry Cadogan, a younger son, so that William would have had to survive on a modest allowance and find remunerative employment. How exactly the young Cadogan earned his keep has not been discovered for certain. There is mention of his having been a sometime soldier of fortune and, in view of his descent and later career, this would appear quite possible.

According to his monument in Christ Church Cathedral, Dublin, and other sources William, a man of 'rare mental endowments', went to Ireland in 1633 as private secretary to Thomas Wentworth the ill-fated Earl of Strafford who had been appointed Lord Deputy of that country by Charles I. No doubt he went with thoughts of improving his position and gaining a fortune. Richard Boyle, later Earl of Cork and clearly a man of some business acumen, had gone to Ireland as a young man in the hope of acquiring cheap land and by 1629 he had a yearly income in rents of £20,000.

As a secretary to the Earl, William Cadogan was well placed both to learn the art of political in-fighting from the older statesman and to benefit from his patronage, as did other members of the Lord Deputy's personal entourage. Strafford was the king's protégé and former President of the Council of the North. During his eight years in Ireland he was to amass a land holding of 57,000 acres and build for himself a mansion house on his Kildare estate.

Against the king's wishes Strafford was executed in May 1641 in the prologue to the English Civil War and it is a little later that William next appears, as a member of the Irish House of Commons, sitting as a 'New English' representative for the borough of Monaghan on a committee seeking to impeach certain of the newly deceased Lord Deputy's former associates.

Earlier in 1641 William's first wife Elizabeth had died and the following year he married again to Elizabeth Roberts of Caernarvon who in that same year gave birth to their only son, Henry.

On 24 October 1641 the indigenous Catholic Irish rose in revolt against their Protestant rulers who promptly withdrew into their walled towns and planter castles to await relief. These were troubled times in Ireland with savagery on both sides and so it is not surprising to find William Cadogan holding a king's commission as an army officer. Captain Cadogan was evidently held in some regard by his superiors. Lord Ormonde, the then Lord Lieutenant General of Ireland, writes in 1645, 'To our trusty and wellbeloved Captain William Cadogan'[1] who some short while afterwards is recorded as the Deptuty Governor of the Castle of Trim in County Meath.

Captain Cadogan, during the ensuing four years, appears like many another military leader to have forsaken the Royalist cause with its ambivalent approach to the Catholic rebels and he next appears having attained his majority in Cromwell's army. Oliver Cromwell landed in Ireland with his main army in August 1649, some six months after the execution of Charles I. He remained nine months and led his New Model Army on a crusade against the rebels; the massacres at Drogheda and Wexford are well documented. When Cromwell departed, the uprising had effectively ended although a further ten years was to pass before the country was administratively quiet.

On the 14 March 1660 Major William Cadogan died at the age of fifty-nine. For his services he had been appointed Governor of the Castle and Borough of Trim; he had become again a Member of the Irish Parliament as well as a man of property, being possessed of a house in St George's Lane,[2] Dublin and an estate in the County of Meath of 411 Irish acres or some 665 acres in English measurement.[3] To understand the devolution of Cadogan's acres it is necessary now to return to the earlier mention of planters and to explain briefly the concomitant 'plantations'.

Henry II was the first English monarch to assert dominion in Ireland and by the early fourteenth century Norman settlers controlled nearly two-thirds of the land. This process was at first checked and then reversed so that in the fifteenth century the area of Norman settlement had shrunk to little more than a beach-head known as the English Pale, a fluctuating area situated around Dublin. There followed a period of passivity on the part of the English towards the Irish until about 1534 when Henry

VIII, fearing that Ireland might be used as a base for Counter-Reformation forces, decided upon a more active programme to subjugate the Irish people comprised of an alliance of native Irish and 'Olde English', as the Anglo-Normans were now known. Henry's policy of surrender and regrant, an attempt to put the local lords into a position of feudal inferiority to the English king, failed. It then gradually became clear that the composite Gaels with their preference for Rome in religious matters would not willingly accept English rule and hence was born, in the reign of Queen Mary, the idea of an implanted English population which perforce necessitated the confiscation of land from the native population. The newcomers were the 'planters' and the land they occupied the 'plantations'.

The plantation policy continued throughout the reigns of Elizabeth and James I and indeed Strafford had been engaged during his time in Ireland in the same policy which brought about the rebellion of 1641: an attempt by the Catholic Irish to repossess their native land. The situation was complicated by the presence in Counties Antrim and Down of a strong Scottish element which had begun to arrive in greater numbers in the early 1600s as the result of the colonising activities of three ambitious Scots, one of whom was James Hamilton, now well entrenched in land formerly belonging to the O'Neills of Clandeboye. It was a direct result of the plantation policy that Major William Cadogan came into possession of his land.

The English Parliament early in 1642 had passed an Act 'for the speedy and effectual reducing of the rebels in His Majesty's Kingdom of Ireland', better known as 'the Act for adventurers'. Essentially the general public were invited to contribute sums of money in exchange for Irish land which by implication would not become available for possession until the rebels themselves were dispossessed. The contributors were the 'adventurers'. It was a grandiose scheme that envisaged a public contribution of £1 million in exchange for 2.5 million acres of Irish land and there was provision for a specific scale of values, so that for example one acre of Ulster was secured on a contribution of four shillings and one acre of Connaught for six shillings.

The adventurers' scheme did not achieve its financial objective although in due time those that did contribute came into possession of allotments of land by way of the Cromwellian settlement which also had to take into account the debentures granted to the army in Ireland. An individual debenture promised the soldier a settlement of his arrears of pay in Irish land rather than in hard cash.

The notional interests of both the adventurers and the debenture holders were assignable and it was by way of an assignment of an adventurers' share for £400 that Major Cadogan became a landowner, drawing in one of the lotteries held at Grocers Hall in London in 1653 and 1654, an estate of 411 Irish acres or 665 English acres in Liscartan Parish, the Barony of Navan in the County of Meath.

The purchase price was not a particularly large sum of money and probably came from the Major's personal savings. His basic pay entitlement in that rank was some £300 per annum and perhaps one or both wives had brought with them a dowry. Additionally, it is possible that by this time both Henry and Catherine Cadogan had died leaving their only child some inheritance. As to whether this primary estate was enlarged by way of a soldier's debenture is unknown. What is certain is that Major Cadogan, unlike many others, had his land confirmed to him by Charles II. Of some 35,000 soldiers meant to be disbanded and settled in Ireland, only some 7500 eventually had their lands confirmed to them following the Restoration. Major Cadogan's will was destroyed along with many other documents during the civil war in Ireland (1922–23). From an earlier extract it is known that the principal beneficiaries were his wife Elizabeth and his only son Henry, then a law student in Trinity College, Dublin.

In the month following William's death there was born, on the 16 April 1660 a son, Hans, to Alexander and Sarah Sloane who lived in County Down some seventy miles north-east from the Cadogan land.

Elizabeth survived William by only five years and her will does exist.[4] It has, as might be expected, a genteel rustic quality, taking care of the servants and disposing of the livestock, and the 'lands, tenements and hereditaments' are bequeathed to 'my dearly beloved son Mr Henry Cadogan'.

Henry Cadogan lived in Dublin and he married, probably in his late twenties, Bridget Waller, a daughter of Sir Hardress Waller, MP, one of the signatories of the death-warrant for Charles I, and hence a regicide who spent some time in the Tower before transportation to Jersey. Bridget's sister Elizabeth was the mother of the 1st Lord Shelburne, one of the executors of the 1st Earl Cadogan who died in 1726.[5] Their lordships were, of course, cousins.

Henry had two daughters, Frances who died aged nine years and Penelope, and three sons. These were Ambrose who died in childhood and is interred alongside his paternal grandfather, William the eventual 1st Earl Cadogan born in 1672 and Charles born in 1685. He had a successful career in the law being at one time, as was his father, the High Sheriff of County Meath. Henry lived a full span before his death in 1714 and he too is buried in Christ Church Cathedral. It appears that Henry substantially increased the family acreage, adding an estate in County Limerick of some 1800 acres including a castle at Adare.

The Liscartan lands and the house in Dublin were sold by Lord Cadogan to his cousin Lord Shelburne in 1719 while a quarter of the land in Limerick together with the castle was disposed of in 1721. The remaining acres were sold by Charles Cadogan in 1729, possibly as part of the unscrambling process of the, by then deceased, 1st Earl's complex financial affairs. Clearly, however, the Irish adventure was the foundation of the Family's fortune.

The Right Honourable William Lord Cadogan Lieutenant General of His Majesty's Forces &c.a

CHAPTER IV

The 1st Earl Cadogan (1672–1726)

William Cadogan was born at Liscartan on the family's Irish estate and after attending Westminster School in London went on in 1686 to study, like his father Henry, at Trinity College, Dublin. His first active involvement with the military was at the Battle of the Boyne in July 1690 when he fought as a boy cornet against the deposed James II with King William's army. Later that year he took part in the sieges of Cork and Kinsale, attracting in the process the attention of John Churchill, later to become the Duke of Marlborough, who was twenty-five years his senior. In 1694 he obtained a commission as Captain in General Erle's Regiment of Foot with which he served under the King in the Flanders campaign.

King William died in April 1702 and a month later Marlborough was put in overall command of the confederate armies against the French in what was to become known as the War of the Spanish Succession, setting up his headquarters at the Hague and taking Cadogan with him as his quarter-master general. Cadogan was to become Marlborough's Chief of Staff and Director of Intelligence and also his personal representative in the House of

Commons where he sat for Woodstock on Marlborough's nomination.

Captain Cadogan had become a major in the Inniskilling Dragoons in 1698 and in 1701 he had been promoted brevet colonel of foot. Following the fall of Liège in 1702 he was rewarded with the colonelcy of the 6th Horse which became famous as 'Cadogan's Horse', nicely described as 'Big men mounted on big horses'.[1] Colonel Cadogan was wounded and had his horse shot from under him during the attack on Schellenburg in 1704. He was nonetheless present at the Allies' victory at Blenheim shortly after and in that same year he was promoted brigadier-general.

The year was a busy one for the newly promoted general for at about the same time he took a Dutch wife, Margaretha Cecilia Munter, daughter of Jan Munter, Lord of the Manors of Zanen and Raaphorst. They had two daughters: Sarah who became the Duchess of Richmond and Margaret who was destined to become Countess Bentinck, daughter-in-law to the Earl of Portland.

The Cadogans' home in Holland was at Raaphorst, an ancient estate comprising a 'castle', more akin to an old English manor house, and 500 acres of land. The estate came to Margaretha in 1711 and she lived there until her death in 1749. In addition to Raaphorst the Cadogans had a second Dutch estate *De Drie Papegaaien* which translates as 'The Three Parrots' and this lay in the same administrative district as the castle. All the Dutch land had been disposed of by 1757 as part of a belated winding-up process of the Earl's estate.

In 1707 Cadogan was promoted major-general and some few months later was accredited Envoy Extraordinary and

Countess Cadogan, wife of the 1st Earl

Raaphorst Castle, Holland

Minister Plenipotentiary to the States of Holland. General Cadogan had not, however, given up active soldiering and, following the battle of Ramillies in 1706, he was also engaged in the battles of Oudenarde in 1708 and Malplaquet in 1709.

William Cadogan's first recorded foray into landed property on his own account was in 1707 when he purchased from one James Tyrrell the Manor of Oakley and other land in Buckinghamshire, comprising a 'mansion house' and some 373 acres of mainly pasture land. This estate was vested in trust for William's brother Charles by way of a Private Act of Parliament.[2] It then passed to Sarah, Duchess of Marlborough, again probably as part of the unravelling process of William's financial affairs which was found to be

The Manor House, Oakley, Bucks today

necessary following his death. The manor house remains standing today in well maintained condition.

In 1712 Marlborough fell from royal favour and both he and Cadogan went into exile in Holland. As a result Cadogan was called upon to resign his offices and employment under the Crown. Their virtual banishment lasted until the Hanoverian succession in 1714 in which Cadogan played a very active part. With George I on the throne he was reinstated in his former rank of lieutenant-general, a rank he had achieved in 1709. He was also rewarded with the lucrative appointments of Master of the King's Robes, Lieutenant of the Ordnance and Colonel of the Coldstream Guards. Additionally he was re-chosen as Member of Parliament for Woodstock and was again accredited as Envoy Extraordinary and Minister Plenipotentiary to the States-General of Holland.

Also in 1714, General Cadogan took from Elizabeth, Countess Dowager of Kildare a lease for 99 years of a mansion house 'commonly called Caversham Lodge' set in Caversham Park along with a stock of deer and 12 acres known as Reading Meadow. The house was situated very near Reading and was conveniently placed for access to the royal courts in London and Windsor and to Marlborough's palatial residence at Blenheim. The lease provided for an annual rent of £200 together with 'One Brace of Fat Bucks and One Brace of Fat Does'.[3]

There then followed a tour of duty as Commander-in-Chief of the Forces in Scotland early in 1716, stamping out what remained of the Jacobite uprising, and this resulted in General Cadogan being ennobled as Baron Cadogan of Reading in the summer of that same year. In the September came Cadogan's crowning diplomatic achievement when, as Ambassador Extraordinary to the Hague, he signed the Treaty of Defensive Alliance between Great Britain, France and Holland.

The matter of General Cadogan's enoblement was mentioned by him in a letter dated 23 February 1716 to the Duke of Marlborough addressed from Aberdeen.[4] 'Your Grace having been pleased to order me to let you know the names of the Barony I desire to be called by . . . the place I propose is called Cadogan near Wrexam on the borders of Wales, of the Cheshire side . . .' The general's intelligence on this occasion appears to have been at fault for there was no such territory called 'Cadogan' sufficient to support his proposed title. General Cadogan seems to have confused 'Plas Cadwgan', which is translated as 'Cadogan's Hall', with a 'place . . . called Cadogan'. Plas Cadwgan was a magnificent massively timber-framed late medieval stone-built house only demolished some ten years ago. It was sited on the western side of Wrexham in Denbighshire in what is today the County of Clwyd. At the time of General Cadogan's letter the house was in the ownership of the Myddleton family and had been since the early seventeenth century. In view of its antiquity however, it is quite likely that at one time the house was in possession of a member of the Cadogan family.

In April 1718 Lord Cadogan acquired the freehold interest of his Caversham estate together with additional land from the trustees of the Earl of Kildare for £6200. The Countess Dowager's interest had been for her life only. This estate now extended to some 1000 acres of again largely pasture land. A Private Act of Parliament was necessary due to the Earl having bequeathed a life interest in this and other properties to a son of Charles II by the Duchess of Portsmouth, the 1st Duke of Richmond. This Duke's son, the eventual 2nd Duke, was to marry Lord Cadogan's daughter Sarah. Interestingly, the County of Kildare in Ireland is bordered to the north by the County of Meath, where at that time part of the Cadogan Irish estate still lay, now vested in Lord Cadogan following the death of his father Henry in 1714.

Sarah (née Cadogan), Duchess of Richmond, with her husband, the 2nd Duke of Richmond

In May 1718, some few weeks following his purchase of the Caversham freehold, Lord Cadogan was created Baron Cadogan of Oakley, Viscount Caversham and Earl Cadogan, County Denbigh with a special remainder of the barony only, failing a male heir, to his brother Charles. It appears that by this time Lord Cadogan must have acquired land in County Denbigh, although details of this acquisition have yet to be discovered.

Lord Cadogan clearly intended Caversham to be his power base and by 1723, only three years before his death, he had demolished the old house and built in its place what was by all accounts a magnificent mansion with columned porticoes, set in gardens landscaped to a grand design which included two canals, tree-lined walks, lawns and flower beds, all sweeping down to the River Thames. There was much statuary and according to a contemporary description the estate was 'one of the noblest seats in the Kingdom'.[5] There seems little doubt that the rebuilding of Caversham was Lord Cadogan's financial undoing; he is reputed to have spent £130,000 on the project, a sum which today would be equivalent to some £5.5 million. In addition to this expense, Sarah's dowry cost him £60,000 and when he died he was maintaining two houses in London: one in Jermyn Street and another in Piccadilly. Unfortunately and surprisingly no sketch or detailed painting of the mansion house is recorded.

Of Lord Cadogan's remaining years the chief event was the very sad affair of being sued by Sarah, the waspish Duchess of Marlborough, on behalf of the Duke who was by then an old man in frail health, in respect of a sum of £50,000 which the duke had entrusted him to invest in the Dutch funds. Cadogan on his own initiative had instead, thinking it the better course of action, invested the money in Austrian securities which subsequently deteriorated badly. As a result of Sarah's law suit Cadogan was obliged to make good the difference, causing him a heavy loss. Churchill comments that 'Marlborough's brave and faithful comrade, always lax in money matters, had great difficulty in making the necessary restitution.'[6] The commander and his general appear to have had a hand-in-glove relationship and it seems unlikely that this incident would have arisen without the intervention of the Duchess who had written that Lord Cadogan had 'a passion for money beyond anything' she had ever known.

The 1st Earl Cadogan who died at the comparatively young age of 54 was clearly a man with a huge appetite for life. He had accumulated a vast fortune and spent it in addition to his patrimony. He was much criticised, but perhaps this was the inevitable price of his close relationship with Marlborough and the Whig cause and his phenomenal success as soldier, statesman and diplomat. The French ambassador reported in 1724 that 'the immense wealth he (Cadogan) has acquired, and his having, by means of the powerful influence of the Duke of Marlborough, passed over the head of many of his seniors in the army, have drawn on him a great many enemies'.[7]

Lord Cadogan was buried at night, as was then the custom, in the Duke of Ormonde's vault in Henry VII's chapel in Westminster Abbey.

During his last illness the 1st Earl was attended by a well-known physician of the day, Sir Hans Sloane, forbear of the present Earl Cadogan.

CHAPTER V

Sir Hans Sloane (1660–1753)

Hans Sloane was the youngest of seven children, all boys, born to Alexander and Sarah Sloane on 16 April 1660 in County Down, Ireland, possibly in the town of Killyleagh, possibly in the nearby town of Lisnagh.

Only three of the boys lived to adulthood and all achieved a fair measure of material success. James, the eldest son, became a Member of Parliament and an eminent lawyer, whilst brother William became an affluent merchant landowner. Newsletters at the time of his death in 1728 reported his personal fortune at about £100,000.

According to a census of 1659, Alexander Sloane was chief landowner in the barony of Kinelarty with eleven Irish and eleven English and Scots tenants and at about that time he also owned the townland of Lisnagh (now Lisnaw) and other properties. There is circumstantial evidence to suggest that Alexander's forbears were Scots emigrés from Galloway and it was perhaps the shared national origin that led to his appointment as Agent to the Hamilton family, initially to Lord Clandeboye and subsequently to his son, the eventual 1st Earl of Clanbrassil. Alexander is described in a Muster Roll of the time as Quarter-Master in the Clandeboye regiment and after the Restoration in 1660, the year of Hans' birth, he became a Commissioner of Array, an official responsible for choosing able-bodied men as conscripts for the royal service. Hans' father was therefore of the minor gentry and it was perhaps the Hamilton patronage which assisted all three brothers in the early stages of their respective careers, more especially as Alexander Sloane died in 1666 when James was eleven, William eight and Hans but six years old.

There is little certain knowledge as to the origin of Alexander's wife Sarah (nee Hicks) other than that she went from England to Ireland around 1642 with Anne the eldest daughter of Henry Carey, Earl of Monmouth and, interestingly, wife of James Hamilton, Viscount Clandeboye, who was later created the previously mentioned 1st Earl of Clanbrassil.

Killyleagh town is situated on the shores of Strangford Lough and a census of 1659, the year before Hans' birth, shows a modest population of 175 residents of which 126 were English and Scots. The town possessed a school founded and to some extent funded by the Hamilton family.

Latin was taught at the school and in view of the fact that both elder brothers were one-time pupils it is assumed that Hans duly followed suit. The name 'Hans' derives from Johannis, the Latin form of John; Sloane derives from the Caledonian-Celtic O'Sluaghain.

In his youth Hans suffered from tuberculosis, an illness which effectively confined him to his room for three years until in 1679 at the age of nineteen he left Ireland to study medicine, first in London then in Paris, before taking the degree of Doctor of Medicine at the University of Orange in the South of France in 1683.

During his first stay in London the young Sloane also studied botany at the Physic Garden in Chelsea, an association which was to prove life-long and no doubt to some extent influenced him in his eventual purchase of the Manor of Chelsea in 1712 from William Cheyne, the 2nd Viscount Newhaven.

Once qualified, Sloane was fortunate enough to obtain a letter of introduction to Dr Thomas Sydenham, the most eminent physician of the day and it was with his assistance that Sloane set about becoming an eminent practitioner in his own right. In 1687 he was admitted Fellow of the College of Physicians and that same year he accompanied the Duke of Albemarle as his personal physician to Jamaica, where the Duke was to take up his appointment as Governor. Sloane had arranged an excellent financial package for himself: a £300 advance for medical equipment and a salary of £600 a year. He then displayed some business acumen by investing his savings in a supply of quinine which presumably he was able to use to advantage once in the tropics. The newly appointed Governor was already in ill health before leaving England and in the year following his arrival he died. Sloane had meanwhile in addition to attending upon the Duke been caring for other patients, including Sir Henry Morgan, former pirate and ex-Governor of Jamaica.

In 1689 Sloane accompanied the Duchess when she left Jamaica for London. On arrival he took up residence at the Duchess's house as her personal physician and he retained this appointment for the next five years, leaving at about the time of his employer's marriage to Lord Montagu. The Duchess was both wealthy and socially well-connected;

Sir Hans Sloane

coming of the Cavendish family, her father was the Second Duke of Newcastle who owned land in thirteen counties and whose income in 1715 grossed £32,000. Undoubtedly Sloane owed to her in great part his subsequent rise as the fashionable physician, a calling which enabled Sloane both to build up a renowned collection of books and curios and to purchase the Manor of Chelsea and other property.

Sloane did not permit his improving position to blunt his commercial edge and when he gave the College of Physicians a loan of £700 he did so at 6 per cent interest. It should be noted, however, that he also made a present of £100 to the College and when the loan was repaid he entertained his fellow physicians at dinner.

Six years after his return from Jamaica in 1695, Sloane married Elizabeth Langley, daughter of a London Alderman and widow of Dr Fulk Rose of Jamaica. No doubt Sloane had gained the acquaintance of the Rose family during his service with the Duke of Albemarle. The former Mrs Rose was a rich woman. It is reported that Dr Rose's plantations brought him £4000 a year, one-third of which was devised to his wife. The settlement on her marriage to Sloane secured to her the sum of £10,000. Lady Sloane, as she eventually became, died in 1724, predeceasing Sloane by some 29 years.

Sloane's practice flourished and he attended upon both Queen Anne and her consort Prince George of Denmark, obtaining from him a fee of £100. Sloane's professional time generally was reckoned to be worth a guinea an hour so that, allowing for his more illustrious patients, his gross income must have been in the order of £3500 per annum.

In 1712 Sloane purchased the Manor of Chelsea initially for use as an occasional country retreat and later as his retirement home and a museum for his magnificent and varied collections including 50,000 books, 32,000 medals and coins and some 300 paintings and drawings.

Sloane resided in and practised from a house in Bloomsbury on the Bedford Estate which he rented for £8 14s per annum, and it was from here that he continued to attend upon the Royal family. In 1714 he was one of the physicians who attended Queen Anne in her last illness and two years later he was created a Baronet by George I. Sir Hans' star remained in the ascendant and in 1722 the first Hanoverian monarch appointed him Physician General to the army, a post he held for the next five years. In 1727, now 67 years of age, he was appointed Physician in ordinary to George II and elected President of the Royal Society. One of his first acts from the Presidential chair was to call in subscriptions in arrear whilst another was to persuade the Council to enlarge the scope of their investment portfolio, including the purchase of some fifty acres of land in rural Acton which in due time paid a handsome dividend.

Chelsea had clearly not lost any of its early attraction for Sir Hans and in 1737 he purchased Beaufort House in Cheyne Walk from the Duke of Beaufort for £2500. This mansion had once been the home of Sir Thomas More and had been described as 'the Greatest House in Chelsey'.[1] In 1740, much to the dismay of many, Sir Hans had the house demolished. Sir Hans was in his eighty-first year when in 1742 he retired from practice and made the final removal from Bloomsbury to the Manor House at Chelsea, taking with him his collections which he enjoyed for a further eleven years prior to his death and burial at Chelsea Old Church in 1753. He had lived to see his ninety-third year, a not inconsiderable feat for the eighteenth century.

In his Will the former Court Physician and man of property put the value of his collections at £50,000. As a result, however, of an Act of Parliament passed in June 1753 these collections were purchased for the nation, by way of a lottery, for the newly formed British Museum at a cost of

Kip's view of Beaufort House, left of centre, 1708

£20,000. The Manor of Chelsea was devised by Sir Hans between his two daughters, Lady Cadogan and Sarah Stanley.

Although the will of Alexander Sloane is now lost, it appears that at his death the family house in Killyleagh was bequeathed to pass ultimately to the eldest son, James, with the residue landed property devised to the three sons equally. In 1715 William's son, another William, bought out the interests of his late Uncle James in the family's County Down lands for £1200. Assuming this sum to have included the house at Killyleagh, it seems likely that Sir Hans' share of the family landed estate would have been valued at something in the order of £1000.

The story of Sir Hans Sloane is not therefore one of progression from poverty to great wealth. He was born into comfortable circumstances and like many another of his time and background he used patronage and marriage, combined no doubt with earnest application and much ability, to amass his personal fortune.

The Manor of Chelsea, 1753

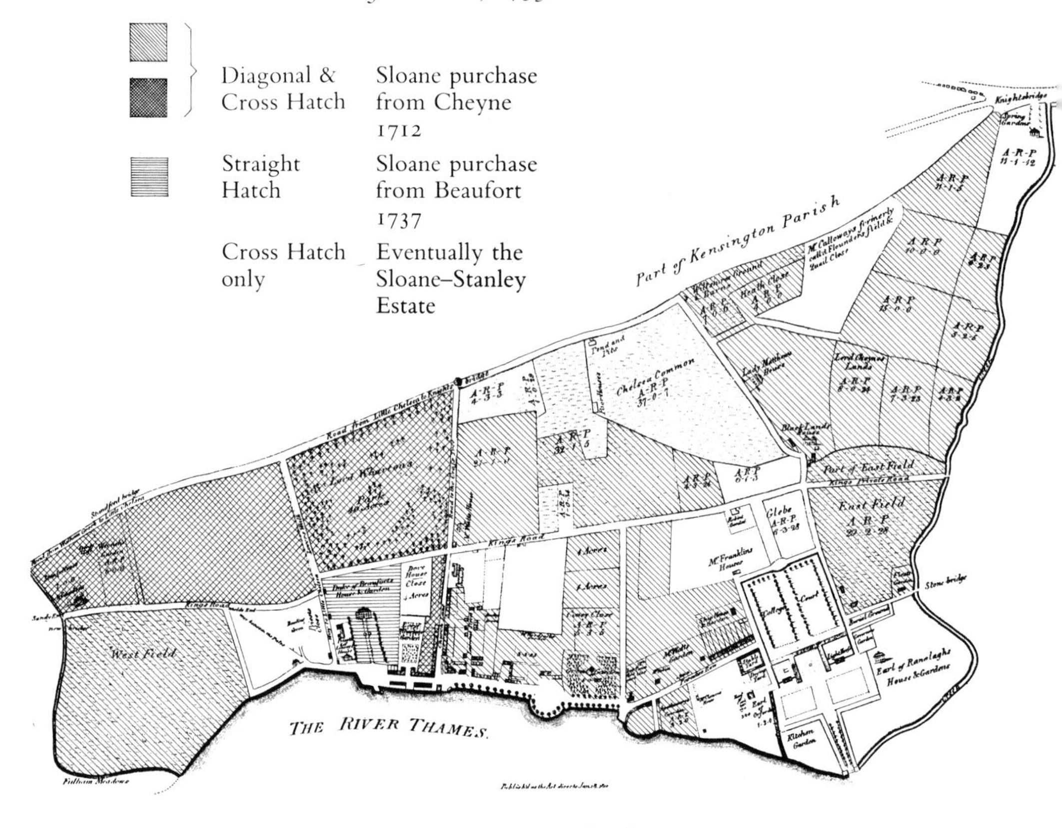

CHAPTER VI

The Manor of Chelsea

A manor has been defined as 'a district of land of which the freehold was vested in the lord of the manor, of whom two or more persons, called freeholders of the manor, hold land in respect of which they owed him certain free services, rents or other duties.'[1] With the extinguishment of manorial incidents in 1922, manors have ceased to exist.

The name 'Chelsea' probably derives from the Anglo-Saxon place name current in the year 785 'Cealchyoe' where 'cealc' is translated as 'chalk' and 'hyo' as 'a hithe, wharf, landing place'. Given the nature of the local soil however, perhaps the name refers to a 'hithe' where chalk or lime was landed for some unascertained purpose. Over the years the name has changed to 'Chelchod' in 1197, 'Chelcheth' in 1291, 'Chelshith' in 1535, 'Chelsey' in 1610 and finally the contemporary spelling circa 1754.

The first mention of the Manor of Chelsea appears in the reign of Edward the Confessor (1042–66) when it was given by Thurstan, the governor of the King's palace, to the Abbot and Convent of Westminster. William the Conqueror by a charter dated at Westminster, then confirmed the land to the Monastery of Westminster. Domesday book, completed in 1086, mentions the lands in Chelsea as in possession of the Church of Westminster and so they

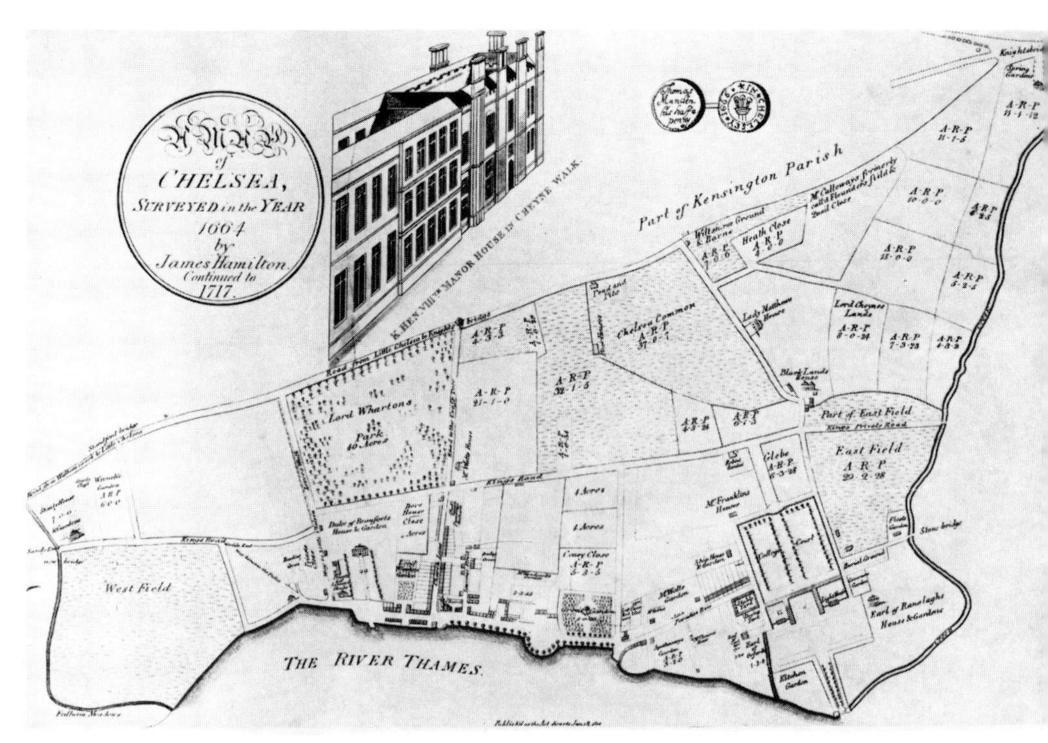

Hamilton's map of Chelsea

remained until Gervace, Abbot of Westminster, assigned the 'Manor of Chelchithe' to his mother, Dameta, and her heirs. Afterwards it was held by the heirs of Bartholomew de Fontibus. Little is then recorded of the manor until in the reign of Henry VII (1485–1509) Sir Reginald Bray is found in possession. The manor then devolved upon Sir Reginald's niece Margaret who married Sir William Sandys, afterwards created Lord Sandys.

In 1536 Lord Sandys exchanged with Henry VIII the Manor of Chelsea for Mottisfont Priory in Hampshire and the new Lord of the Manor soon set about building himself a new manor house, the river frontage of which occupied what is today the precise frontage comprised in 19–26 Cheyne Walk. The old, rather cramped manor house occupied a site set back from the river in contemporary

Lawrence Street. The King had presumably gained acquaintance with the delights of rural Chelsea, as indeed it then was, when entertained by his Lord Chancellor, Sir Thomas More, at his magnificent mansion further up river called Beaufort House and prior to his execution virtually at the King's behest in 1535.

It was at the new Manor house, a Tudor pink-brick building possibly with a crenellated front not unlike St James's Palace which was built at about the same time, that Queen Elizabeth I (1533–1603) spent her formative years and she appears to have remained there until the death of Catherine Parr in 1548. The manor had earlier been assigned to Catherine on her marriage to the King in 1543.

The manor was then bestowed successively upon the first Duke of Northumberland, his son the Earl of Warwick, and then again upon the Duke who was beheaded in 1553 following his attempt to place upon the throne Lady Jane Grey who had herself stayed at Chelsea. The Duchess of Northumberland then lived at the manor house until her death three years later at which point Anne of Cleves, who after her divorce from Henry had remained in England, appears to have taken up residence. However, she died a few months later.

Queen Elizabeth then leased the manor in 1559 to Ann Duchess of Somerset. Her occupation was rather longer than the previous two Ladies of the Manor and she died twenty-eight years later in 1587 thereby restoring the reputation of Chelsea's recuperative airs. The manor was then granted to the eventual Lord Stanhope of Harrington followed by a further grant by the Queen in 1591 to Catherine, Lady Nottingham, first wife of the Lord High Admiral.

There are several records of the Queen coming to dine at the Manor house with the Lord Admiral at this time. Lady Nottingham died on 25 February 1603 and was buried at 'Chelsey' on 21 March, three days before the death of the Queen.

James I subsequently granted the manor to the second Lady Nottingham and during her lifetime it was disposed of to Sir John Monson and Robert Goodwin, Esquire who subsequently sold it in 1638 to the Duke of Hamilton's Trustee. The Duke in the following year obtained a grant from the King of the manor in fee and proceeded to enlarge the manor house by making a large self-contained addition to the western end, thereby nearly doubling the river frontage, which subsequently was sold separately by Lord Cheyne in 1664 as a residence for the Bishops of Winchester, being known as Winchester House. The Duke of Hamilton not surprisingly followed the royalist banner in the Civil War and having suffered the misfortune of being taken prisoner at the battle of Preston, then suffered the greater misfortune of being beheaded on 9 March 1649.

The manor and manor house were among the lands made forfeit by Parliament in 1653; the house only being later sold by the appointed Commissioners to one John Walker and others. After changing hands more than once the house was finally conveyed by the heirs of the Duke of Hamilton to Charles Cheyne, Esquire in 1657 who acquired the whole manor three years later. Lord Cheyne, as he became, lived in the eastern or old end of the manor house. He died in 1698 and was succeeded by his son William, Lord Cheyne who does not appear to have lived in the house for very long. According to the old rate books the house was then let to various personages until 1710 after which it appears to have lain empty until the manor was purchased by Sir Hans Sloane in 1712.

Appurtenant to the manor was a share in Chelsea Common which was eventually built-over in the early nineteenth century. Hitherto the Common had been used for various purposes including the grazing of animals, gravel extraction and the drilling of militia.

Sir Hans did not come to live at Chelsea until 1742 and in the meantime the house had been let for varying periods. He had intended the house to become a museum for his great collections but this was not to be and regretfully, following Sir Hans' death in 1753, the manor house for all its two hundred and seventeen years of rich history was pulled down to make way for a new development.

CHAPTER VII

The 2nd Baron Cadogan of Oakley (1685–1776) and the 1st Earl Cadogan (New Creation) (1728–1807)

The 1st Earl Cadogan was succeeded in 1726 in the barony of Oakley by his brother Charles who was then in his forty-first year and a colonel in the 4th Foot. The 1st Earl's other titles lapsed in the absence of a male heir.

Although a long-serving army officer and a politician like his brother, Charles does not appear to have possessed the same élan and he probably owed much of his early advancement to William's patronage. He was, for example, Whig MP for Reading (1716–22) and for Newport, Isle of Wight (1722–26) where William held the governorship. A diarist writing in 1717 describes Charles as 'a loose person of no great income'[1]. Charles is recorded as having served as cornet in Colonel Rooke's Regiment of Foot in Flanders and he was present at both Oudenarde and Malplaquet. In 1715 he was commissioned lieutenant-colonel in the Coldstream Foot Guards and two years later he married Elizabeth Sloane, the younger daughter of Sir Hans Sloane

2nd Baron Cadogan of Oakley

Lady Cadogan, wife of the 2nd Baron

at the church of St George the Martyr in Queen Square. In 1719 Charles rose to the rank of colonel and thereafter his promotional progress through the upper echelons was steady but unremarkable, aside from the fact that he did not achieve general's rank until 1761 when he was 76. It is evident from his later career that he was in favour with the monarchy and in 1747 he is noted as having accompanied, along with other members of the aristocracy, King George II when, attended by the Prince of Wales, he reviewed Sir Robert Riches' Dragoons in Green Park.

In 1731 Lord Cadogan had a house at 49 Albemarle Street, moving to 17 Bruton Street in 1742 where he remained until 1762. This is the house where Queen Elizabeth II was born in 1926 although unfortunately it was later demolished. In 1763 he moved to 3 New Burlington Street where he remained until his death in 1776. (It is worth

17, Bruton Street

Mrs Francis Cadogan, first wife of the 1st Earl of the New Creation

noting that street numbering did not in fact begin until early in the nineteenth century.) In the latter part of Lord Cadogan's life there was a Cadogan House, known alternatively as Chelsea House, in Chelsea situated where today stands the Duke of York's Headquarters. Quite how this house fitted in with the other town houses is unknown. Perhaps Cadogan House was essentially the family manor house from which the Estate was administered with the other houses being used for more fashionable entertaining.

Caversham was Lord Cadogan's sole country home and it appears from a guidebook published in 1761 that with the death of William, Charles set about reducing the size of the mansion house 'as less regarding the outward Glare of Magnificence than Use and Convenience'.[2] All was not economy however and Lord Cadogan retained the services of the celebrated Lancelot 'Capability' Brown to landscape the parkland leading down to the river. This prompted a contemporary observer to write that 'By taking down some and leaving conspicuous the most noble (trees), made it one of the finest parks imaginable . . .'[3] By all accounts and notwithstanding the alterations made to the house by Charles, the family seat was a handsome one. It is sad therefore to record that the house was burned down in 1850. The present house on the same site was constructed in 1852 and now houses the BBC's Monitoring Station. A sweep of parkland remains including some of the cedars of Lebanon planted by Lord Cadogan and with a little imagination one can envisage Caversham's former magnificence.

Lady Cadogan gave birth to a son and heir, Charles Sloane Cadogan, in 1728 and at the early age of 21 he became a Whig MP for Cambridge, a seat he held for twenty-seven years.

Charles Sloane married in 1747 at St George's, Hanover Square, Frances Bromley daughter of Henry Bromley, the 1st Baron Montfort. This was an ill-starred union and five of six sons all pre-deceased their father. Lord Montfort committed suicide in 1755 and in 1768 Frances Cadogan 'dyed raving mad'[4] only four days after the death of her mother-in-law, Lady Cadogan.

Lord Cadogan survived his wife by eight years and when he died in his ninety-second year he was the senior general in the army. He is buried at Caversham together with Lady Cadogan and Frances Cadogan.

The new Lord Cadogan was therefore a wealthy widower in the prime of life, with a much admired country seat

Cadogan House in Whitehall

and a fine town house, Cadogan House in Whitehall. It was hardly surprising therefore that in the year following his father's death he married again. His bride was Mary Churchill, a kinswoman of the Duke of Marlborough and grand-daughter of Sir Robert Walpole, the 1st Earl of Orford (1676–1745), usually considered to be the first prime mininster.

At the time of this second marriage Lord Cadogan was Master of the Mint, a valuable sinecure which three years earlier according to Horace Walpole, Sir Robert's son, had netted him some £30,000 when the light guineas were called in for recoining.

Of the union Walpole, famed for his correspondence, wrote that 'My niece's match with Lord Cadogan, since she

Downham Hall, Suffolk

herself approves it, gives me great satisfaction. She is one of the best and most discreet young women in the world, and her husband, I am sure, is fortunate.'[5] For some unknown reason Lord Cadogan appears at a later date to have upset Walpole who then describes him as 'the complete toady'.[6]

The marriage, which produced three sons and two daughters, ran into difficulties after only six years when Lady Cadogan appears to have become enamoured of a local vicar, the Reverend Cooper. Lord Cadogan, in an effort to save the situation, then virtually overnight sold Caversham and removed his wife and family to a new home at Downham Hall, Santon Downham in Suffolk. 'In consequence of some unhappy connubial events, the . . . Earl (Cadogan) sold land, house, furniture, wine in the cellar, and, if we are to credit report, the very roast beef on the spit, to Major Marsac, for a sum of money one day before dinner'.[7]

Downham Hall was a rather sombre looking pile when compared with Caversham, standing in some 6000 acres. The estate was bisected by the River Ouse so that part lay in Norfolk and the rest in Suffolk. Not surprisingly it had its own fishery. The Hall was demolished by the Forestry Commission in 1923.

In addition to Downham Hall Lord Cadogan had another country home at nearby Merton Hall in Norfolk which he leased in 1787 from Lord Walsingham. He retained the tenancy certainly until 1804 and it seems likely that he did so until his death. Most of the house was burnt down in 1954.

Lord Cadogan's marital problems unfortunately were not over and in 1796 at the age of sixty eight he divorced Lady Cadogan, citing the Reverend Cooper.[8] Although a

Merton Hall, Norfolk

Whig politician, Lord Cadogan was a supporter of Pitt's government and as a result in December 1800 he was created Viscount Chelsea and Earl Cadogan. The newly created Earl Cadogan lived another six years before dying at Downham Hall in 1807. He was succeeded by Charles Henry Sloane Cadogan, the eldest and sole remaining son of his marriage to Frances Bromley.

The Santon Downham estate was sold in 1825 and Cadogan House in Whitehall, sold in 1808 by Lord Cadogan's executors, was pulled down around 1950 to make way for what is now the Ministry of Defence building. The government building incorporates in its basement part of King Henry VIII's wine cellar which earlier formed part of the ground floor of Cadogan House.[9]

1st Earl Cadogan of the New Creation

CHAPTER VIII

Estate Development in the Eighteenth and Early Nineteenth Centuries

The creation of the Cadogan Estate came about with the death of Sir Hans Sloane in 1753. It had previously been set in train by the marriage of his younger daughter Elizabeth to Charles Cadogan in 1717, a union of the Sloane landed wealth with the Cadogan aristocratic and political power.

By way of a codicil to an earlier will Sir Hans bequeathed one moiety or one half of the Manor of Chelsea to Lady Cadogan and her heirs and the other moiety to her elder sister Mrs Stanley and her heirs. Initially therefore the manor lands were under the joint control of both families. By 1821, however, one-half of the Stanley moiety had reverted through bequest to the 2nd Earl Cadogan which together with his own inheritance gave him, or to be more precise his trustees, direct control over three-quarters of the old manor lands, an area of some 270 acres ripe for development due to a westwards expansion of property development generally in London. The remaining quarter share in the physical land division passed to Sir Hans' great-nephew Hans Sloane who assumed the Stanley name in 1821 to become Hans Sloane-Stanley, so giving rise to the Sloane-Stanley Estate in western Chelsea.

The interest in Chelsea Common was also shared, probably on the basis of 20 per cent of the whole going to the Cadogan family with a 10 per cent share to the Stanley family. The Estate, presumably by way of purchase, had increased its share to 50 per cent by 1833.

Chelsea at this time presented very much the rural scene with an abundance of orchards and vegetable market gardens. The River Thames was fished for salmon, roach and pike and the river was very busy with plying craft, often tying-up by Cheyne Walk. The population was about 3000 accommodated in some 450 houses. It was an ideal retreat for those, like Samuel Pepys in 1663, in search of fresh air and relaxation.

Hence, no doubt, Sir Hans Sloane's purchase of the Manor in 1712. His purchase of Beaufort House in 1737 appears to have been commercially motivated, for the house was much run-down and the site was, in theory at least, suitable for development. The house was demolished at the instruction of the Lord of the Manor in 1740 but it was not until 1750 that he granted a long lease of the land to Count Zinzendorf and the Moravian Brotherhood with a view to their constructing a religious settlement. This plan came to nought however and circa 1770 the Moravians started letting-off the ground as building plots to form the present-day Beaufort Street. A small area of the original grant remains, in the Moravian burial ground lying at the back of Beaufort Street. Sir Hans had also been busy in the direct development field and at about the same time as he purchased Beaufort House he had built on the 'Great

Garden' of the Manor House the first eighteen houses of Cheyne Walk and the southern end of Chelsea Manor Street. The development of Cheyne Walk was continued following his death and upon the demolition of the Manor House to provide a further eight houses.

The commercial development process had therefore already been started by Sir Hans some time before his death. With the Cadogan family in control, initially in

Henry Holland

concert with the Stanley family, this process gradually gathered a greater momentum.

In 1771 negotiations were started with Henry Holland the architect and son-in-law of Lancelot 'Capability' Brown for a lease of some ninety acres of land stretching from Knightsbridge to just south of Sloane Square upon which he intended to build a new town, 'Hans Town', comprising in the main simple four or five storey houses which would appeal to the upper-middle and professional classes. Building was delayed due to the war with America which started in 1775 and the death of the 2nd Baron Cadogan in 1776. In 1777, however, an agreement was completed with the 3rd Baron Cadogan and work appears to have begun at once with the first houses included in the rate books for 1779.

Hans Town was the forerunner for other new towns including Agar Town, Camden Town, Canning Town and Kentish Town although none of these had the same social pretensions. The name of Hans Town fell into disuse in late Victorian times but a number of the old boundary bollards marked 'Hans Town', may still be seen around the neighbourhood. One is sited outside the Danish Embassy in Sloane Street.

Apart from the houses in Sloane Square and those on the west side of Sloane Street, Holland also constructed Hans Place as a suitable entry point for his own mansion house which he built on a twenty-one acre site set aside for the purpose. 'Sloane Place' or 'The Pavilion' as the house became known was of timber construction dressed in Welsh slates. The southern elevation incorporated Ionic columns and it was subsequently suggested by some that

Thompson's map of Chelsea, 1836

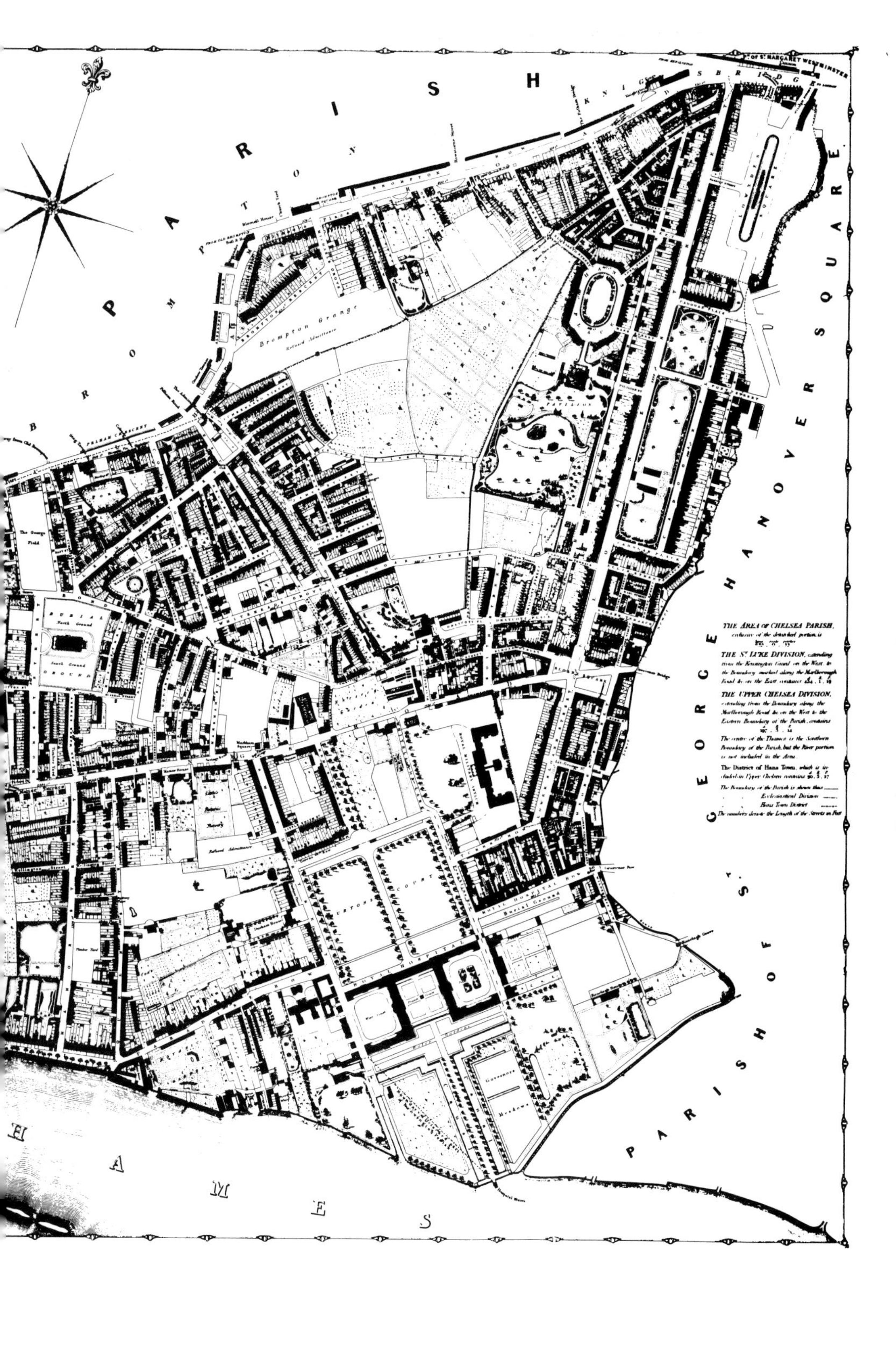

B R O M P T O N P A R I S H
K N I G H T S B R I D G E
OF ST MARGARET WESTMINSTER
L O W N D E S S Q U A R E
P A R I S H O F S T G E O R G E H A N O V E R S Q U A R E
T H A M E S
BROMPTON
Brompton Grange
Refused Admittance
FULHAM ROAD
The George Field
BURIAL GROUND
North Ground
South Ground
PAVILION
BURTON'S COURT
ROYAL HOSPITAL
Burial Ground
Governors Meadow
THE AREA OF CHELSEA PARISH,
exclusive of the detached portion, is
THE St LUKE DIVISION, extending
from the Kensington Canal on the West to
the Boundary marked along the Marlborough
Road &c. on the East contains
THE UPPER CHELSEA DIVISION,
extending from the Boundary along the
Marlborough Road &c. on the West to the
Eastern Boundary of the Parish, contains
The centre of the Thames is the Southern
Boundary of the Parish, but the River portion
is not included in the Area.
The District of Hans Town, which is included in Upper Chelsea contains
The Boundary of the Parish is shewn thus
Ecclesiastical Division
Hans Town District
The numbers denote the Length of the Streets in Feet

139, Sloane Street, a Holland House

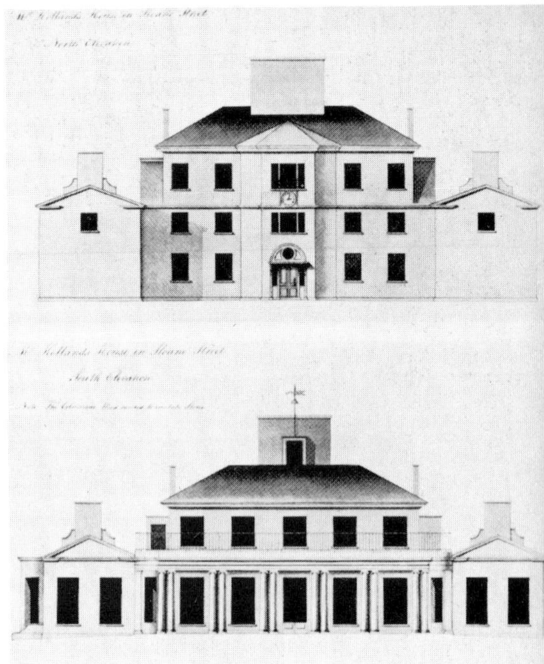

'The Pavilion'

Holland's house was a model for the Pavilion at Brighton which he designed for the Prince Regent in 1787. The garden to the house was naturally enough laid out by Holland's father-in-law and included a serpentine lake with an island, lawns, ornamental trees and an ice house in the form of a Gothic ruin.

The houses on the east side of Sloane Street were also built by Henry Holland. As far as Cadogan Place is concerned, however, only the north, north-east and south terraces appear to have been constructed by him with the remainder – now stucco-fronted houses with columned porches on the south-east terrace – having been built by William Whitehead a little later and possibly after Holland's death at Sloane Place in 1806.

Henry Holland had originally intended to construct a

Cadogan Square – north side. Site of the Pavilion, with reminiscent colonnade

church on what are today the Cadogan Place gardens, but this plan came to nought seemingly as a result of some unholy bickering between the local incumbents as to the likely effect upon their respective congregations. The northern garden was subsequently laid out by Humphrey Repton the renowned landscape gardener and the southern garden from 1807 became Salisbury's Botanic Garden.

At the end of the eighteenth century and as a result of the wars with the French the old Cadogan House, situated in the Kings Road just off Sloane Square, was disposed of to the Crown and it was then demolished to make way for the Royal Military Asylum or, as it was more familiarly known after its founder, the Duke of York's School for the children of soldiers' widows.

In about 1809 the Lords of the Manor, the local Rector and the other proprietors let Chelsea Common on building leases only then to discover that the leases were defective due to one of the proprietors being under age. There was also some doubt as to whether the local Rector could bind his successors. A Private Act of Parliament was therefore obtained to rectify the situation.[1]

The early years of the nineteenth century were very busy ones for the Estate. Jubilee Place was built to mark George III's Jubilee and in 1825 Private Acts of Parliament were obtained to facilitate generally the grant of building leases[2] and specifically to demolish Winchester House[3] with a view to development of the site which some five years thereafter provided the houses at the southern end of Oakley Street

123, Sloane Street, a Holland House

Oakley Street

Oakley Gardens

and a further four houses to complete the eastern terrace of Cheyne Walk. At about the same time Cadogan Street was being built and Wellington Square laid out, soon to be renamed Trafalgar Square and subsequently Chelsea Square.

St Luke's church in Sydney Street designed by James Savage was one of the first churches in England in the Gothic revival style and was consecrated in 1824. Following the earlier abortive attempt by Henry Holland, Holy Trinity church in Sloane Street designed by the same architect was completed in 1831.

The nature of Chelsea was changing rapidly and the first two decades of the century each saw a fifty per cent increase in population. There was an inevitable decline in agriculture with only 87 families engaged in it by 1831 compared with 275 families ten years earlier.

A commentator writing in 1829 said that 'It is intended to form a communication with Lord Grosvenor's new magnificent [Belgrave] Square by means of a street [Lowndes Street] to run parallel with the north-east corner of Cadogan Place. By this means Chelsea will obtain a direct connection with London, and henceforth it must be considered as part of the great Metropolis of the British Empire.'[4]

CHAPTER IX

The 2nd (1749–1832) 3rd (1783–1864) and 4th (1812–1873) Earls Cadogan

Very little is known of Charles Henry Sloane Cadogan, the 2nd Earl. He was baptised in 1749 at St George's in Hanover Square, the church in which his parents were married, and as a young man he served as an officer in the army. He then appears to have succumbed to the insanity which marked his mother and maternal grandfather with the result that his affairs and those of the Estate were managed until his death in 1832 by trustees appointed following the issue of a Writ de Lunatico Inquirenda in 1801. The trustees were Hans Sloane (later known as Hans Sloane-Stanley), Horatio Lord Walpole, Charles Churchill, no doubt a relation of the Earl's step-mother, and one William Dickenson of Somerset.

The 2nd Earl Cadogan is noted as a sometime resident in Enfield and there he died, unmarried, at the advanced age of 83 years. He was buried at St Luke's Church in Chelsea.

The heir to the earldom until 21 June 1813 was Lieutenant-Colonel Henry Cadogan, the eldest son of the 1st Earl's second marriage to Mary Churchill. On that day

2nd Earl Cadogan

Colonel Cadogan died at the Battle of Vittoria in Spain, the last major battle of the Peninsular War against the French. The Marquis of Wellington, later raised to ducal rank, wrote 'We accordingly attacked the enemy yesterday and . . . the allied army under my command gained a complete victory; having driven them from all their positions, taken from them one hundred and fifty one pieces of cannon, four hundred and fifteen waggons of ammunition . . . and a considerable number of prisoners.'[1]

Colonel Cadogan led the 71st Highlanders and in the course of the fighting alongside the Spanish allies storming the heights of Puebla he 'received a ball in the groin; he fell and was immediately surrounded by some of his men, and lifted up by them, in order to be removed to the rear; the 71st was then about to apply to their old friend the bayonet, ready for the charge; their Colonel lay in the arms of two soldiers, the balls showering from the hills. "Stop! stop!" said he; "don't take me away until I see the men charge". It was done and gallantly uphill too; the Colonel cheered, as well as his failing voice would allow, and his last moments were blessed with the smile of victory.'[2] In the heroic manner of the age his last words were 'I trust to God that this will be a glorious day for England'.[3]

Colonel Cadogan was also courageous in his private life. In 1809 he fought a duel with Lord Henry Paget (later the Earl of Uxbridge and Marquis of Anglesey) on Wimbledon Common to protect the reputation of his sister Lady Charlotte Wellesley, sister-in-law of Arthur Wellesley the eventual Duke of Wellington. Lady Wellesley, a mother of four young children, had earlier shocked London society by eloping with Lord Paget, a married man, in a hackney carriage and perhaps understandably the Paget family regarded her as a 'nefarious damned Hell-hound' and a 'maudite sorcière'.[4] All appears to have ended happily however when the two elopers in due time became united in matrimony.

There is a memorial to Colonel Cadogan in the gallery of St Luke's Church in Chelsea together with a number of tablets commemorating other members of the Cadogan family.

St Luke's Church, Chelsea

With the death of Colonel Cadogan the heirdom passed to his younger brother George who by that time was a very successful captain in the Royal Navy. George Cadogan was born at 14 St James's Square in 1783 and at the age of 13 entered the Senior Service. He became a lieutenant in 1802, a commander in 1804 and he was promoted to post-rank in 1807. Admiral Cadogan as he became

for twenty years of his professional career saw much active service. He served in the *Indefatigable* at the capture of the French frigate *Virginie*, in 1796, and at the destruction of the *Droits de l'homme* in 1797. He was mate of the *Impetueux*, commanding the barge to lead the fire ship in the attack of the combined French and Spanish Squadrons in Aix Roads, in 1799. He took part in the expedi-

3rd Earl Cadogan with his dog Fen

138, Piccadilly

tion to Ferrol; and was at the capture of Guepe in 1800. As Lieutenant of the *Lede* he was in action with the Boulogne flotilla, was Commander of the *Cyana* at the capture of the French privateer brig *Bonaparte*, and of the *Ferret* at the capture of a Spanish brig of 14 guns. As Captain of the *Pallas*, in the Walcheren expedition, he also rendered much useful service and when Captain of the *Havannah* he took and destroyed within ten months ninety-one sail of vessel, mostly armed. Lord Cadogan commanded the same frigate at the reduction of Zara in 1813, and that may be considered the crowning action of his naval career.[5]

The fortress at Zara in what is now Yugoslavia, with some 110 guns and 18 howitzers capitulated to the combined Austrian and English forces after sustaining a cannonade of thirteen days from the English batteries. In his official report to the Admiralty the commanding admiral wrote that 'The judgement, perseverence, and ability shewn by Captain Cadogan, on every occasion, will not, I am persuaded, escape their Lordships' observation. With the crews of a frigate and a sloop he has accomplished as much as required the squadron united at Trieste.'[6]

Captain Cadogan was made a Knight of the Austrian Order of Maria Theresa in 1813 for this exploit and the following year he received recognition at home in being awarded the Companionship of the Bath. Four years earlier Captain Cadogan married Honoria Louisa Blake, sister of the 1st Lord Wallscourt and by her had four sons and two daughters. Lady Cadogan pre-deceased her husband and died in 1845 at Wiesbaden. It is unrecorded as to when Lord Cadogan's pet dog, Fen, given to him by the writer Sir Walter Scott, passed away. It is known however that he was 'honourably buried in the Rectory garden' situated in Old Church Street.[7]

The family home in London was at 138 Piccadilly which Captain Lord Cadogan leased in or about 1833. The house was built in 1798 and was remodelled in 1891 with giant pilasters.[8] It remains standing and is presently occupied by a commercial undertaking.

In September 1831 Captain Cadogan was appointed an extra Naval Aide-de-Camp to William IV and at about the same time he was, during the lifetime of his half-brother the 2nd Earl Cadogan, created Baron Oakley of Caversham. Six years later, by which time he had succeeded to the earldom, Lord Cadogan was appointed Naval Aide-de-

Camp to Queen Victoria. He attained Flag-rank in 1841, was promoted vice-admiral in 1851 and finally became a full admiral in 1857. Admiral Lord Cadogan had lived a full and adventurous life, much in the mould of C.S. Forester's fictional naval hero Hornblower, when in 1864 at the age of 81 he died at his house in Piccadilly.

The admiral was succeeded by his eldest son Henry Charles Cadogan, then aged fifty-two, a pale scholarly figure by comparison who had graduated from Oriel College, Oxford in 1832 when he was twenty years old.

Henry, Viscount Chelsea as he was then, went on to a diplomatic and political career as Attaché at St Petersburg in 1834–35, Conservative MP for Reading 1841–47 and for Dover 1852–57, then back to the diplomatic corps as Secretary of Embassy at Paris in 1858–59.

In 1836 the heir to the earldom married his first cousin Mary Sarah, third daughter of the Honourable and Reverend Gerald Valerian Wellesley by Emily Mary, daughter of the 1st Earl Cadogan and Mary Churchill. Gerald Wellesley was brother of the Duke of Wellington. Lord and Lady Chelsea acquired in 1850 a large mansion house at 13 Cadogan Place, referred to in later rates books as 28 Lowndes Street, and this became the new Chelsea House. It was built in 1807 for Lady Sarah Napier and it remained the family's town home until its demolition by the 5th Earl Cadogan in 1874.

Following his succession to the earldom in 1864 the new Lord Cadogan appears to have taken up occasional residence at Wood Rising Hall in Norfolk, the country home of the new Viscount Chelsea who leased the Hall from John Weyland from 1866 until 1873. Lady Cadogan died in

4th Earl Cadogan

February of that year and Lord Cadogan died at Wood Rising only some four months later to be succeeded by his eldest son, George Henry Cadogan. The first cousins were buried together in what was the family vault at St Luke's Church. The rector of the day recorded that on '8 June Earl Cadogan died at Lord Chelsea's home in Norfolk. After his burial the vault was for ever closed.'[9] This was not to be, however, and in 1969 the Cadogan coffins along with others were removed to a sealed communal area within the crypt to make way for a youth club. May they now rest in peace. The Cadogan vault with its heavily studded timber door surmounted by the family coat-of-arms survives and is used, disappointingly, as a storeroom.

CHAPTER X

The 5th Earl Cadogan (1840–1915)

George Henry Cadogan was the eldest of the four sons of the 4th Earl and his wife Mary. He was born at Durham where his maternal grandfather was Prebendary at the Cathedral and christened at St James's in Westminster.

George Henry, or Viscount Chelsea as he was styled, was educated at Eton and in 1857 he was one of four boys chosen to accompany the Prince of Wales and three tutors on a walking tour of the Lake District and later on a European holiday to Germany, France and Switzerland. Lord Chelsea and the Prince, the future King Edward VII, were to remain life-long friends. The other three boys were to become William Gladstone MP, son of the eventual Prime Minister, the 16th Earl of Derby and the 2nd Viscount Halifax.

From Eton Lord Chelsea went on to Christ Church, Oxford and in 1865 he married Lady Beatrix Jane Craven, fourth daughter of the 2nd Earl of Verulam. They had six sons and two daughters. The eldest child, Albert Edward, was born in 1866. Lady Beatrix 'was, in her girlhood, a hard and daring huntress, whose prowess was often proved in the annals of the Craven Hunt,' and this passion for the hunt remained with her life-long.[1]

5th Earl Cadogan and his wife

In May 1873 Lord Chelsea was elected Conservative MP for Bath but had to stand down the following month on succeeding to the earldom – surely one of the shortest periods of representation in the House of Commons. With an eye to a grander style of living than his father or perhaps with the thought in mind of a continuance of his political career the new Lord Cadogan soon retained the services of William Young, the architect who was to design the War Office in 1898, to build a new Cadogan town house. As a result Chelsea House was rebuilt on its old site at the eastern end of the north terrace of Cadogan Place. It was completed in 1874 when Lord Cadogan was Under Secretary for War under Disraeli. Chelsea House was a most imposing stone-built structure on basement to 4th floor levels with a magnificent L-shaped Louis-Seize drawing room cum ball-

Chelsea House, Cadogan Place

room on the first floor measuring overall seventy feet by fifty-five feet and an equally magnificent dining room on the ground floor measuring forty-four feet by twenty-one feet. The house with its white marble hall had twenty-one rooms, the servants' quarters being in the basement and the attic, with a spacious stable at the rear where were kept the carriage horses and the park hacks for the mandatory rides in nearby Rotten Row. When the family was in residence, usually only during the season of May, June and July each year, a staff of thirty members was necessary to maintain the household in its various pursuits. In its heyday the house had 'Prodigious, astounding, and unexpected beauties on a noble scale. Sumptuous magnificence and gold-gleaming splendour meet the eye at every turn; but the prevailing impression is that it is a place full of slumberous peace, too infinitely reposeful to be categorised'.[2]

In 1878 Lord Cadogan moved from the War Office to become Under Secretary for the Colonies and in that same year Lord and Lady Cadogan suffered the loss of their eldest son Albert Edward who died at Chelsea aged eleven. The new heir to the earldom was Henry Arthur Cadogan, also called Viscount Chelsea, born in 1868. Lord Cadogan's career progressed and in 1885 he was appointed a Privy Councillor, becoming Lord Privy Seal with a seat in Lord Salisbury's cabinet the following year, an office which he held until 1892. He was responsible for Irish business in the House of Lords.

During this period the family's country home was at Babraham Hall in Cambridgeshire, a red-brick and stone Jacobean style mansion of about thirty rooms with mullioned and transomed windows, gables and a big square asymmetrically placed tower. It was built in 1829 and enlarged in 1864, and Lord Cadogan leased it from the Adeane family until 1889. The house remains and it is now used by the Agricultural Research Council, a far cry from the Victorian era of the private railway saloon and fashionable house parties.

The 5th Earl Cadogan's younger son Sir Edward Cadogan recalled the evening at Chelsea House of 22 June 1887, Queen Victoria's first Jubilee year, when the queen 'exhausted by the strenuous round of functions imposed on her beforehand,' deputed Lord Cadogan to entertain her guests to dinner. 'It took a whole army of men working all day to transform the great white marble hall . . . into a bower of palms and exotics. The long gilded ballroom on the first floor was improvised as a banquet hall – more ornate and capacious than the dining room in common use.' The guests at dinner that evening with the Blue Hungarian Band playing softly in the background included the Prince

Babraham Hall, Cambridgeshire

and Princess of Wales, the King of Greece, the Duke of Sparta, King Humbert of Italy, the King of Saxony, Prince William of Prussia, the Crown Prince Rudolph of Austria, King Carlos of Portugal, the Grand Duke Serge of Russia, the King of Belgium and the King of Denmark. As Sir Edward remarks, 'rarely have the representatives of so many foreign dynasties met round one table in a private dwelling.'[3]

In 1889 Lord Cadogan left Babraham Hall and purchased Culford Hall near Bury St Edmunds in Suffolk. The porticoed mansion house with 400 acres of parkland and 11,000 acres of sporting land was built by the 1st Marquess of

Culford Hall, Suffolk

Cornwallis about 1790 and evidently it lacked sufficient accommodation for Lord Cadogan's needs. He immediately arranged for his architect William Young to prepare plans for its enlargement and when these were executed the house provided a spacious 51 bedrooms, 15 bathrooms, 11 reception rooms and staff accommodation. Lord and Lady Cadogan were then able to entertain on a grand scale. In November 1903 the Prince and Princess of Wales (later King George V and Queen Mary) stayed at Culford for a week's shooting and in December 1904 King Edward VII and Queen Alexandra also visited Culford.

It was during their transfer from Chelsea House to Culford in the early 1890s that the family archives were destroyed by a fire in the removal van which had been parked overnight in London: an irretrievable loss of many vital and interesting documents.

For some while past a confidant of Queen Victoria, Lord Cadogan was made a Knight of the Garter in 1891 and in 1895 he was elected as member for Chelsea of the newly formed London County Council. This office was short lived for later that same year he was appointed Viceroy of Ireland (as Lord Lieutenant), an interesting return to a country in whose history the family already shared. This was not altogether a sinecure for only thirteen years earlier the sensational Phoenix Park murders in Dublin, close to the Viceregal Lodge, occurred when Lord Frederick Cavendish and Thomas Burke, Chief and Under Secretaries of Ireland, were assassinated by the Fenians, an anti-British secret association dedicated to overthrowing English rule in Ireland. Lord Cadogan remained in Ireland until 1902 and his viceroyalty, given the difficult background, was considered a success.

On his return to England Lord Cadogan divided his time between Chelsea House and Culford, managing his estates. He was by no means entirely the urban man and with large flocks of Suffolk and Southdown sheep he was regarded as one of the country's leading flockmasters. His country tenantry appeared content although, as might be expected, this was not always the case in Chelsea, more particularly when it came to redeveloping parts of the Estate.

In addition to his other interests Lord Cadogan also enjoyed the Turf and in 1879 his horse Mazurka won the Stewards' Cup at Goodwood and the Coronation Stakes at Ascot. His only classic winner was Lonely who won the

Oaks in 1885, 'but Goldfield was so close to victory in the Two Thousand Guineas of 1882 that Lord Falmouth, the owner of Galliard, who actually caught the judges' eye first, turned round to Lord Cadogan in the stand and congratulated him on his success'.[4]

In 1907 Lady Cadogan died and was buried at Culford. The following year Lord Chelsea died of cancer aged forty and two years after this his only son Edward died aged seven after an operation for appendicitis. The heirdom then passed to Lord Cadogan's third son, Gerald Oakley Cadogan, born in 1869 and the father of the present Earl Cadogan.

The deceased Lord Chelsea had four daughters one of whom, Alexandra Mary, married the 10th Duke of Marlborough in 1920, so further uniting the two ancient families whose forebears had fought together at Blenheim and other historic battles. The duchess died in 1961, also of cancer, and her eldest son John is the present duke.[5]

In 1911 Lord Cadogan married his cousin Countess Adele Palagi at Florence, a union which was to last only four years before his death in 1915. He is also buried at Culford together with Lady Cadogan.

Lord Cadogan was regarded as 'a clear-eyed, level-headed, straight-forward gentleman, with frank manners and firm convictions, who has ever seen his duty with clear vision and done it thoroughly'.[6] His outward style of living with his many royal and noble friends was opulent and is unlikely to be repeated in today's more egalitarian, some would say grey, society.

CHAPTER XI

Redevelopment in the Late Nineteenth Century

Primary development was carried out by the Estate as and when the opportunity arose throughout the nineteenth century. To the east of Queen Street (now Flood Street) in 1839 the 3rd Earl Cadogan had built Elizabeth Street (now Christchurch Street) and Caversham Street with their own church which was consecrated Christchurch. In the 1860s in the time of the 4th Earl Cadogan, Redesdale Street, Redburn Street, Tedworth Square and the southern end of Radnor Street (now Radnor Walk) were built on former nursery land. The area around First Street, Hasker Street, Ovington Street and Walton Street was built up in the mid 1840s.

Chelsea generally continued to change and by 1861 the population had grown to almost 60,000 reaching a peak in 1897 of 75,380. It has been falling for most of this century and now stands at around 40,000. The building of the Embankment started in 1858 and by the time it was completed in 1874 Chelsea was effectively separated from the river which had once given it so much of its distinctive character. Chelsea Bridge was opened in 1858 with a new road connecting it to Sloane Square; Albert Bridge at the

Tedworth Square

First Street

south end of Oakley Street was completed in 1873. The Sloane Square underground station was opened in 1868.

Property development is perforce a cyclical process and when Henry Holland's lease came to an end in about 1874 the land and more particularly the 21-acre site occupied by Sloane Place in Hans Town was ripe for redevelopment. Part of the land attaching to Sloane Place had been leased some years earlier to a Mr Prince who erected a sporting club there for use in connection with a cricket field which he had leased from the adjoining owners, Smith's Charity. The charm of Sloane Place, once Holland's pride and joy, had long since faded and at the end it had been divided into smaller units, the death-knell of many an old property. Generally in late Victorian times Holland's houses were considered old-fashioned and those north of Hans Place and south of Sloane Square were suffering from multi-occupation, that bane of an estate owner's life when old leases are due to come to an end.

In 1874 Mr North Ritherdon, a builder from West Hackney, signed an agreement with the 5th Earl Cadogan to demolish Sloane Place and cover what had been Holland's private land with houses 'not inferior to those in [nearby] Lowndes Square', which were very attractive houses built by Thomas Cubitt. Part of the agreement provided for the builder to link up Pont Street with what is now Beauchamp Place, so giving direct access from Belgravia to Brompton Road. A local Act of Parliament enabled the builder to acquire those houses on the west side of Sloane Street which would have to perish in the cause.

Mr Ritherdon's interest subsequently lapsed and he was replaced as the developer by the Cadogan and Hans Place

Estate Ltd, a company formed for the purpose and whose chairman was Colonel W.T. Makins MP, a respected businessman who had 'modern' ideas in the matter of architecture. Hitherto the acme of architectural perfection in London, to many, was the stucco finish familiar in Belgrave Square and Eaton Square. Colonel Makins, however, was a devotee of the red brick and so came about what one commentator has tartly described as the 'frowning canyons of bilious red brick' of the Cadogan Estate.[1]

The new Cadogan Square was to be the jewel in the crown of the development and some of the early houses completed in 1878 were designed for particular tenants. Most of the square, however, was sub-leased in parcels to other developers who were permitted to choose their own architects. Trollope and Sons built the north and east sides, save one house, together with parts of Pont Street in accordance with a design prepared by their own architect, George Robinson. The south side was also developed as a whole, to the designs of J.J. Stevenson while the west side, which perhaps is the most visually interesting, was designed by various architects including R. Norman Shaw (numbers 68 and 72) and Lord Cadogan's architect William Young (numbers 56 to 60). Shaw, the leading exponent of the 'Queen Anne style', was later the architect for Scotland Yard (1890) and the Piccadilly Hotel (1908).

The building of Cadogan Square took ten years to complete and number 61, which was finished in 1879, was one of the earliest high-class apartment buildings erected in London. The central garden of the Square as at present arranged was laid out in the spring of 1886. Redevelopment continued southwards and Draycott Place was completed in 1893 followed by both Cadogan Gardens and Culford Gardens in 1897.

The evolution of the retail shop was generally a gradual process and Chelsea was no exception. Holland, for example, had originally built houses in Sloane Street and Sloane Square and some of these would have been occupied by the milliners, glove-makers and others, as a necessary adjunct to the well accoutred members of the aristocracy and upper classes of nineteenth-century society. Retailers such as these eventually came to realise the commercial benefits to be gained from having a ground-floor shop window and accordingly the building which started life as a simple house evolved into a mixed use of a shop on the ground floor with

Cadogan Square – East side

Cadogan Gardens

the upper floors given over to fitting rooms, workrooms and storage with perhaps accommodation for the proprietor. This effective change of use was of course long before Town and Country Planning measures came onto the statute book.

Purpose-built shops appeared in Chelsea in the middle of the nineteenth century and in 1858 it is reported that, 'At the south-western angle of Sloane Square . . . a large block of shops and houses has just been erected . . . that forms a great improvement as contrasted with the very inferior buildings with which they are immediately associated some of which are . . . of the most miserable description . . . The shops are being fitted with every modern improvement [including] revolving shutters.'[2]

The private house thus began to disappear in Sloane Square, although the residential element was maintained with, for example, the construction by the Estate's retained developers of Cadogan Mansions in 1895. Peter Jones' department store opened in 1889 on Estate land. The process was a little slower in Sloane Street.

The Holland lands north of Hans Place and south of Sloane Square with their multi-occupied and run-down houses were also considered by the Estate to be suitable for redevelopment. This resulted in the construction of Sir Herbert Stewart's Herbert Crescent in 1891 and the building by William Willett of Lower Sloane Street, Sloane Gardens and Holbein Mews at about the same time. Willett, apart from being a fine builder, is remembered as a leading advocate of daylight saving which eventually came into being with an Act of Parliament in 1916.

The late nineteenth century was a developer's bonanza

and of course what was good for the developer was equally beneficial for the Estate and for the neighbourhood generally. In 1889 'The Mansions' at No. 1 Sloane Gardens were completed to a design by Edwin T. Hall, one of the architects of Cadogan Square, followed shortly afterwards by the completion of Sloane Court East and Sloane Court West where the architects were Messrs Rolfe and Matthews. A reporter of the day comments that 'So great a change has been made here that no one who visited the district four or five years ago would know it. Narrow streets of squalid houses have given place to wide avenues of mansions.'[3]

The old Holy Trinity church in Sloane Street was demolished in 1888 and a new church designed by J.D. Sedding built with considerable financial assistance from the 5th Earl Cadogan was consecrated in 1890. Four years

Herbert Crescent

1, Sloane Gardens

later the Royal Court Hotel was built in Sloane Square. The Royal Court Theatre was rebuilt in 1888 and was designed by Walter Emden and W.R. Crewe.

This general upheaval and redevelopment of course caused problems for those poorer tenants perforce dispossessed and the Estate fully recognized its social responsibilities in this respect by, for example, donating land to the Guinness Fund Trustees for the construction of cheap rented dwellings. This particular gesture which necessitated buying-out a sitting lessee was estimated to have cost the Estate some £40,000. The initiative for redevelopment did not always come directly from the Estate and in Turks Row for example it was the local Vestry which in effect started the process through insisting upon the closure of the existing houses.

Royal Court Hotel, Sloane Square

CHAPTER XII

The 6th (1869–1933) and 7th (1914–) Earls Cadogan

Gerald Oakley Cadogan, the 6th Earl Cadogan, was like his father educated at Eton. He was a professional soldier and served initially as a lieutenant in the 1st Life Guards, later serving with the 3rd Battalion of the Suffolk Regiment with the rank of captain.

Captain Cadogan served as Aide-de-Camp to his father during the time of the 5th Earl Cadogan's viceroyalty in Ireland and afterwards he went on to serve with the Mounted Infantry in the second Boer War from 1900 until its end in 1902. At the age of forty two Lord Chelsea, as he was then styled, married Lilian Eleanor Coxon and some four years later in 1915 he succeeded to the earldom. Lord and Lady Cadogan had three children: Beatrix Lilian Ethel, Alexandra Mary and William Gerald Charles, the present Earl Cadogan.

Following the death of his father Lord Cadogan did not take up residence at Chelsea House but remained at his own smaller house at 33 Grosvenor Street.[1] The old family town house was then leased to Sir Owen and Lady Mai Philipps. The house in Grosvenor Street, fortunately still standing but now used as offices, is structurally a Georgian house

6th Earl Cadogan

33, Grosvenor Street

built in 1725 whose facade was completely refronted in stone in 1912 notwithstanding protests from the neighbouring tenants. It is nicely proportioned, four windows wide and four storeys high with some fine internal features including a stone staircase from ground to first floors with elegant Georgian wrought iron balustrading.

The 6th Earl resided at 33 Grosvenor Street until 1928 when he removed across the road to the smaller 48 Grosvenor Street[2] and here he lived until his death in 1933 at the comparatively early age of sixty-four. No. 48 Grosvenor Street no longer remains as a private house. It was incorporated with the adjoining 47 in 1938/39 and is now, like so many other formerly fine houses in Mayfair, used for commercial purposes.

At Culford life went on much as before with Lord Cadogan taking as keen an interest in the running of the estate as had his father. The 6th Earl Cadogan was an informed naturalist and bird watcher and he made a list of over ninety different types of bird which he had seen in the grounds. He was also prominent in sporting circles being chairman of the British Olympic Council and President of the Chelsea Football Club. Perhaps it is not surprising that he did not aim to emulate his father's way of life on the political stage.

All was to change at Culford, however, shortly following the succession to the earldom of William the 7th Earl Cadogan who had not yet attained his majority on his father's death; he was nineteen and, continuing what was becoming something of a tradition in the family, he too had been educated at Eton.

The death of the 6th Earl Cadogan presented the serious problem of death duties to the Estate and as a result the Culford estate was broken-up in 1934 and sold to various purchasers including the Forestry Commission. The mansion house stood empty for some while until being acquired for its present use as Culford School.

The new Lord Cadogan went on to the Royal Military College at Sandhurst, now the Royal Military Academy, and in 1934 he joined the Coldstream Guards. In 1936 Lord Cadogan transferred to the Supplementary Reserve to enable him to devote more of his time to the management of the Estate and he joined the Royal Wiltshire Yeomanry. He served with them throughout World War II in the Middle East and Italy, being awarded the Military Cross at the Battle of Alamein. Lord Cadogan retired as lieutenant-colonel in 1946 when the Territorials were demobilised.

In 1936 Lord Cadogan had married the Honourable Primrose Lilian Yarde-Buller. There were four children by this marriage before it was dissolved in 1960: Sarah Primrose Beatrix, Daphne Magdalen, Caroline Ann and Charles Gerald John, the present Viscount Chelsea. In 1961 Lord Cadogan married Cecilia Hamilton-Wedderburn.

Lord Cadogan has given much of his time to public service and in 1954–59 he was a member of Chelsea Borough Council. In 1964 he was elected the last Mayor of Chelsea before its incorporation with the Royal Borough of Kensington which was particularly apposite as in 1900 his grandfather the 5th Earl Cadogan had been elected Chelsea's first mayor. With the death of Sir Hans Sloane in 1753 and the establishment of the British Museum, each Lord Cadogan from the 2nd Baron Cadogan of Oakley onwards (except for the 2nd Earl Cadogan) was an hereditary trustee of the Museum, including the present Lord Cadogan. The continuity has now been broken, however, with the abolition of hereditary trustees and they are now government appointments. Although the Anglican church would perhaps wish it otherwise, Lord Cadogan remains the patron of the livings at Holy Trinity and St Luke's and he is also joint patron of Old Church, Chelsea – the sole remaining privileges of the 'Lord of the Manor'.

Lord Cadogan, in his seventy-third year, is now virtually retired although together with Lord Chelsea he maintains an active interest in the administration of the Estate. He spends his time between his homes in Cadogan Square and Perthshire in Scotland, interspersed with visits to his sheep farm near Perth, Australia.

7th Earl Cadogan

Viscount Chelsea

CHAPTER XIII

The Estate in the Twentieth Century

After all the intense activity during the closing years of the nineteenth century, the opening years of the new century were comparatively quiet.

The Estate has for various reasons during the course of its history sold parcels of land of varying size. In 1902 it sold a dilapidated and poorly planned twenty-acre site to The Cadogan and Hans Place Estate (No. 3) Ltd who in 1929 in turn sold the land to the shipping magnate Sir John Ellerman. The site, which comprised the greater part of the old Chelsea Common, was bounded by Fulham Road and what are now known as Draycott Avenue, Elystan Street and Elystan Place and contained some 750 dwellings.

In 1906 William Willet completed the massive brick and stone building on the south side of Sloane Square which still bears his name. Amos F. Faulkner was the architect. Shops occupied the ground floor with twenty-four flats on the six floors above. Each flat was served by a passenger lift and had a drawing room, dining room, four bedrooms, kitchen, pantry, bathroom and three water-closets. They were much sought after, as the modern flats of their day.

Sloane Street was the scene of further redevelopment

activity at the end of 1924 when numbers 30–33 at the corner of Hans Crescent were pulled down and a new building erected in the early months of 1925. This now houses amongst others the Aston Martin showroom and a branch office of Coutts Bank. In April 1925 numbers 9–16 were also demolished and Knightsbridge Court was erected on the site, a building subsequently lost to the Estate.

In 1932 the early nineteenth-century houses in Trafalgar Square (now Chelsea Square) were pulled down and new houses erected in their place to designs by D'Arcy Braddell and Humphry Deane. It was said at the time that the existing houses were 'nondescript' and 'could not be altered satisfactorily to suit modern needs'.[1] Sloane Street was also undergoing further change and new blocks of flats were appearing. In 1931 for example Hugo House at numbers 177–178 was built to provide eleven residential flats and four shops. Chelsea House finally succumbed to a changing world and it was demolished in 1935 to make way for a comparatively anonymous block of flats, bearing the same name, with shops on the ground floor built to the overall design of Thomas Tait, the architect for the *Daily Telegraph* building in Fleet Street erected in 1928. In 1937 a new house was built at 30 Burnsall Street and at about that time eleven new houses were completed in Astell Street together with others in Flood Street.

The previous year had seen a new store erected for Peter Jones in Sloane Square, an architectural success still much admired for its curtain walling, thin mullions and centrally pivotted.windows and for the design of the splay corner on the Kings Road side. The architects were Slater & Moberly with consulting architects C.H. Reilly and W. Crabtree.

30, Burnsall Street

There was comparatively little serious bomb damage caused to the Estate during the Second World War. A few houses only were lost in Chelsea Square, Flood Street, Shawfield Street, Caversham Street, Christchurch Street, Christchurch Terrace, Cadogan Lane, Herbert Crescent, and Sloane Court East.

After the war it was not until the late 1950s that any new

Chelsea Square

Peter Jones, Sloane Square

redevelopment proposals of a substantial nature got under way and then parts of Dovehouse Street and Old Church Street were rebuilt. In 1961 the prestigious Carlton Tower Hotel was built and in the same year the Estate constructed Liscartan House at 127/131 Sloane Street, a commercial building on seven levels, shops on the ground floor with offices above, with a floor area of some 50,000 square feet. Behind the main building, in Pavilion Road, the development provided two mews flats over four garages. The architects were J. Douglass Mathews and Partners.

In January 1962 the Estate announced its massive redevelopment plan for the area north of Sloane Square which was envisaged as taking forty years to complete at a cost, in terms of 1962 money, of some £20 million. The architects were again J. Douglass Mathews and Partners, on this occasion with Lionel Brett, and the scheme was said to be 'one of the largest conceived in London'.[2] Sloane Square was to have a two-storey shopping block with escalators from street level to pedestrian bridges linking all sides of the square and a twenty-six-storey residential block. In Lower Sloane Street a new residential square was planned with another block of flats, here rising more than thirty storeys. Finally in Pont Street a further tower block was drawn-in along with terraced and mews-type houses. A similar scheme had been put forward in 1960 but did not proceed following an unfavourable response from the planning authorities. The revised plan fared no better and as a result the overall concept was abandoned.

Also in 1962 the Estate sold a freehold development site of an acre in extent at the corner of Cheyne Walk and Oakley Street to Wates Ltd. Here originally stood

Winchester House and, more recently, the Old Pier Hotel. At the same time the Estate was seeking tenders for a 99 years' building lease for the construction of thirteen houses, seven studio flats and fifteen garages in Manresa Road and Dovehouse Street.

In 1962, again, the Estate took majority shareholdings in four companies formed with Edger Investments Ltd, later taken over by the Prudential Assurance, to develop more specifically appropriate properties on the Estate. This was a very fruitful union and as a result in the Sixties Cadedge Investments Ltd and the Cadedge Development Company Ltd built for example Fordie House and Oakley House in Sloane Street, Clunie House in Hans Place and the commercial building at 190–192 Sloane Street. Chedger Investments Ltd and the Chedger Development Company Ltd

Manresa Road

for their part built town houses in Astell Street, Cale Street and at 64–112 Walton Street, as well as a block of shops, offices and flats at 155–167 Fulham Road.

Some twelve months previously Lord Cadogan had set up Cadogan Estates Ltd and this company now held the greater part of the Estate's assets. Lord Cadogan and Lord Chelsea were each left with a small share in their personal ownership. Prior to this Lord Chelsea had directly owned most of the Estate and the switch into a corporate holding was a legitimate device to avoid the payment of death duties.

In 1965 the Estate launched another major proposed development plan. This involved a nine-and-a-half acre site in the western area and included Flood Street, Shawfield Street, Radnor Walk, Redesdale Street, Tedworth Gar-

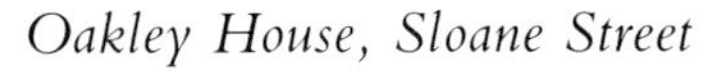

Oakley House, Sloane Street

2, Astell Street

Fordie House, Sloane Str

Walton Street

dens, Tedworth Square, Redburn Street, Tite Street, Christchurch Street and Christchurch Terrace. Most of the leases of the 634 flats and houses concerned expired in 1965 or 1972/73 and it was intended that the scheme be undertaken in two phases to coincide with these dates. The architects for the scheme were Chapman Taylor Partners. The development was to include two tower blocks of flats 33 storeys or 315 feet high, 159 houses and a 3-storey garage to accommodate 294 cars. Overall 385 flats were to be provided. Essentially the idea was to build the tower blocks first and to use these for decanting purposes to facilitate the second phase. There was to be low-rental housing for the poorer tenants displaced.

Strong opposition was encountered to the scheme both from local conservationists and a residents' association and also from the town planners of the Greater London Council who took exception to the two tower blocks which they felt should be reduced to a height of 125 feet. The Estate endeavoured to compromise but there was failure to reach agreement and the result was that the planning department of the Royal Borough of Kensington and Chelsea refused to grant permission for the development.

A public inquiry was held in October 1967 and in May 1968 the Minister of Housing and Local Government announced that the Estate's appeal had failed. Again the two tower blocks, which the Estate considered vital to the scheme, were the sticking point. The Estate therefore was forced to abandon an imaginative scheme and to opt in future for piecemeal development. A further difficulty had in any event been introduced to confound the Estate's plans: the Leasehold Reform Act of 1967. This enabled the lessees of certain houses to compulsorily acquire the freehold interest in their houses, given that certain criteria, including that of a comparatively low rateable value, were met. The freehold of the north side of Tedworth Square and the southern end of St Leonard's Terrace was eventually sold and redeveloped by an outside company.

The Estate had encountered another public inquiry in December 1964 in connection with a proposal to build a car park beneath the north garden of Cadogan Place. The opposition on this occasion came from the London County Council and local residents and was mainly concerned with the loss of mature trees and the fear that the car park would generate additional traffic in the area. The Estate was unable to satisfy the inquiry and a second inquiry was necessary before the two-tier underground garage to accommodate some 349 cars was eventually built in 1968.

In 1972 the Danish Embassy was built in Sloane Street, followed in 1974 by the construction of the luxurious Chelsea Hotel also in Sloane Street, designed by Michael Blampied and Partners. This venture virtually coincided with the property market crash and for some years there was no new development on the Estate, the property developers contenting themselves with the converting and updating of old buildings. They were particularly active in Culford Gardens, Lower Sloane Street and Sloane Gardens, where the old late Victorian leases were falling in for renewal. New developments are again, however, to be seen on the Estate, the latest ones completed being the Pheasantry site in Kings Road which provides a restaurant, shops and offices, Anchor House in Britten Street which comprises 40,000 square feet of air-conditioned office space and the Waitrose supermarket project also in Kings Road. A residential flats redevelopment is pending for the first of the Henry Holland houses in the southern terrace of Cadogan Place, although the original facades will be retained.

And so the redevelopment cycle goes on and will continue for so long as market forces are allowed comparatively free rein.

The Pheasantry Restaurant, Kings Road

CHAPTER XIV

Notable Buildings and Some Famous Residents

Perhaps the most notable building on the Estate architecturally is the Danish Embassy in Sloane Street. Simply put, it looks rather like a large green metal box with rounded edges. It was designed by the outstanding Danish architect Arne Jacobsen shortly before his death in 1971 and it still provokes strong partisan feelings fifteen years on. The only other Jacobsen building in England is St Catherine's College, Oxford which he designed in 1960. The old embassy was in two houses in Pont Street with the ambassador's residence in Cadogan Square. The new building brought the whole organisation under the one roof on a site which had been used as a car park, following the demolition of seven houses on the Sloane Street frontage.

Jacobsen's building is organised on six levels with the ambassador's residence situated on the top two floors, over the embassy offices and overlooking the Cadogan Place north garden. There is a two-storey building at the rear of the site in Pavilion Road for staff accommodation, a service yard at ground and first floor levels between buildings, and parking for 44 cars at ground floor level and in the basement. The height of the main building in Sloane Street

Danish Embassy, Sloane Street

Hyatt Carlton Tower Hotel, Cadogan Place

respects its neighbours and the facade is divided vertically into five bays, recalling that several houses once stood on the site.

Diametrically opposite the Danish Embassy stands the commanding Hyatt Carlton Tower hotel built in 1961 to a design by Michael Rosenauer and occupying virtually the whole of the northern terrace of Cadogan Place where formerly stood ten Henry Holland houses which had been requisitioned by the local authority during the Second World War. It adjoins the block of flats called Chelsea House and has a return frontage along Sloane Street.

The tower block which gives the hotel its name is eighteen storeys high with, to the eastern side, a nine-storey wing. There is a two-storey section to the western side and this is occupied by another branch of Coutts Bank. The main entrance to the hotel is approached by a covered way in Cadogan Place. Faced with Portland stone and with glass fronted balconies the hotel is strategically well placed for Kensington, Mayfair and the West End generally and it has the added advantage of overlooking the well-tended gardens of Cadogan Place. The hotel has two hundred and twenty eight rooms and suites with ancilliary bars, restaurants and lounges and it is luxuriously appointed. At the time of completion it was reported that 'The list of suppliers for the interior of the hotel reads like a catalogue of exhibitors in an International Design Centre',[1] with pictures by Topolski, an Orrefors crystal chandelier and silverware from Georg Jensen. The upper floors offer a splendid panoramic view of the capital's skyline: altogether a building worth visiting.

Just across the way from the Hyatt Carlton Tower,

Hans House, Hans Street

9 Cheyne Walk

tucked away in Hans Street, is Hans House, a particularly attractive late Victorian house built around 1896 in a reddish brick laid in English bond with stone bands and other features including a fine carved stone portico with Corinthian-style pillars forming the main entrance which may be seen through the wrought-iron ornamental gate set in the boundary wall. The steps leading from a small paved garden to the front door are of black and white marble. The house provides four reception rooms, five bedrooms, four bathrooms and a self-contained staff flat in the basement. The entrance hall is particularly spacious, measuring some seventeen feet by twelve feet with a marble floor, panelled walls and a stone fireplace. Double doors lead to a panelled study and further double doors lead into the dining room which overlooks the garden. An L-shaped drawing room twenty-seven feet by twenty-four feet overall is situated on the first floor, with French windows giving onto balconies, together with the library. The second and third floor contain the bedrooms and bathrooms with the kitchen being found in the basement. Hans House is a very fine town house.

No. 9 Cheyne Walk is magnificent. It was built to replace one of the earlier Hans Sloane houses around 1880 on basement to fifth floor levels and the principal rooms have fine views over the Thames with further views of Cadogan Pier and the Albert Bridge. The house is set back behind the gardens of Cheyne Walk and it is surprisingly quiet. It has a paved front garden lying behind a wrought iron gate and railings and a secluded rear garden with a passageway leading to Cheyne Gardens. The house is of red-brick and has two interesting bay windows to the first floor. The accommodation comprises six reception rooms, five main bedrooms, four bathrooms and a self-contained staff flat together with the main kitchen in the basement. The dining room is on the ground floor and has French windows leading onto a rear terrace which in turn leads into the garden. The drawing room with parquet flooring and a fine Louis Quinze marble open chimney piece is again L-shaped and is on the first floor; its two areas measure eighteen feet by twenty four feet and fifteen feet by thirteen feet. The study adjoins the drawing room. On the second floor there are two further reception rooms, a fitted kitchen and a bathroom. The remaining floors comprise, in the main, the bedrooms and bathrooms.

These are but four of the notable buildings on the Estate.

There are many others including 66 Old Church Street which was built in 1936 to the design of the renowned German architect Walter Gropius, and 34 Hans Place with its beautiful drawing room and 'rus in urbe' atmosphere. To treat all these houses, however, would require a separate volume and a further volume would be necessary to describe all those personages who, down the years, have chosen to reside on the Estate. In a book of this nature, one can select only a few in either category and of course the choice is necessarily arbitrary.

Lord Stockton, more popularly remembered as Harold Macmillan the former Prime Minister (1957–63) was born at 52 Cadogan Place on 10 February 1894. It was the home of his parents for nearly fifty years. He recalls that

> Like most of the houses of its type and period, it was tall and thin. The distance from the nursery to the kitchen and basement seemed an infinity. There were, of course,

66, Old Church Street

no lifts, nor [in our house] any back stairs. Everything, including our food and coal, was carried up daily from the bottom to the top. The day nursery looked out over 'the gardens'. These ran between our street and Sloane Street and were a great boon, particularly on hot summer days. Opposite our house was an acacia tree which I liked; also a lamp-post, with the nightly activities of the lamp-lighter. The night nursery faced the mews and immediately behind us was a blacksmith's shop. Among my earliest memories is the noise of the hammer on the anvil which seemed to go on from early morning till late at night – the making of shoes and the shoeing of horses. When we were half-asleep, we could still hear the rumble of the carriages returning from a party, with the ring of the horses' hooves on the cobbles. In our mews there were a few small shops, to which we were not allowed to go, but access to which we sometimes obtained with the help of our cook, who let us out through the back garden. . . At the top of our street was a large mansion, Chelsea House. . . To us humbler neighbours, Chelsea House was a kind of baronial castle only outmatched in importance by Buckingham Palace, to which we were occasionally taken to see the Changing of the Guard. On the steps outside there could generally be seen as we passed a splendid figure, with powdered hair or wig, blue coat, red velvet waistcoat, blue velvet knee-breeches, white or yellow stockings and silver-buckled shoes. This person, who commanded our deepest respect, we firmly believed to be Earl Cadogan himself, proudly surveying his tenants and his properties. [In Sloane Street] some wonderful new shops were being erected, Harvey

33 & 34, Hans Place

Lord Stockton (Harold Macmillan)

Nichols, Woolands, and the like, replacing the old buildings dating, no doubt, from the days when Knightsbridge was little more than a village. Then the crossing – a skilled and dangerous undertaking as the carriages and omnibuses swooped by, at what seemed a breakneck pace. Or else you had to thread your way through one of the great traffic blocks. It is curious to think that people in those days put up with this inconvenience without demur. In the summer a traffic-jam could last two hours or more.[2]

It was to Cadogan Place that Macmillan the soldier returned from the Battle of the Somme during the First World War severely wounded and with his life in danger.

Resolute action by his American mother saved him and of course he went on to pursue an outstanding political career. To the delight of many the voice of Lord Stockton may still be heard, now in the House of Lords. The acacia tree to which Lord Stockton refers, sadly is no more; it was found necessary to fell it at an advanced age some two years ago.

It is not beyond the realms of possibility that as the young Macmillan was being pushed in his perambulator he might have been smiled upon by the much celebrated society beauty Lillie Langtry who lived at 21 Pont Street (1892–97) and then at 2 Cadogan Place (1899–1900). Born in Jersey in 1852 and christened Emilie Charlotte, she was the only daughter among seven children born to Mr and Mrs William Le Breton. Emilie's father was Dean of Jersey and as a child she had been given the sobriquet of 'Lillie' on account of her unusually white skin. In later life she became known as the 'Jersey Lily' after the painting of her under that name by John Everett Millais.

In 1874 Lillie married Edward Langtry and shortly afterwards they came to live in London where the marriage came under much strain with Lillie striving for the gay social whirl and Edward rather more concerned in such outdoor pursuits as fishing. Eventually Edward appears to have become indifferent to Lillie's obvious charms and not surprisingly in 1877 she became the mistress of the Prince of Wales, later King Edward VII. The affair came to an end in 1881 after which Lillie turned her attentions to the stage both in England and America.

In 1892 Mrs Langtry came to live at 21 Pont Street, now part of the Cadogan Hotel, and it was while living here that she lost her jewellery which she valued at £40,000.

Lillie Langtry

Arnold Bennett

Seemingly, when at Pont Street, Mrs Langtry was in the habit of leaving her jewels with a local bank and when they were required she would send her butler to the bank to collect them. On one particular occasion to her horror – for the jewels were not insured – the butler returned to say that according to the bank the jewels were already in her possession. Evidently a thief had misrepresented himself to the bank. The jewels included a large tiara of diamonds and a necklace of sapphires and diamonds. A court action followed and eventually Mrs Langtry obtained £10,000 in compensation from the bank.

In 1897 Mrs Langtry left Pont Street and in 1899, following the death of her husband, she married Hugo de Bathe who was eventually to inherit the family baronetcy. That same year Mrs de Bathe bought 2 Cadogan Place, seven doors distant from Chelsea House. The house was furnished with Louis Quinze pieces and there was a permanent stage in the ballroom for the musicians. Her bedroom was satin lined and on her bed was an eiderdown embroidered with the letters 'ER' for Edward Rex. Mrs de Bathe removed from her house in Cadogan Place, which was one of those demolished to make way for the Hyatt Carlton Tower hotel, in 1900 and no doubt her passing was mourned by the Estate's male inhabitants. The 'Jersey Lily' died in 1929 and at about this time the novelist and playwright Arnold Bennett, living at 75 Cadogan Square, was just starting work on his last completed novel *Imperial Palace*.

Enoch Arnold Bennett was born at Hanley in Staffordshire on 27 May 1867. His father was a draper who subsequently qualified as a solicitor, so giving to Bennett and his two brothers and three sisters a solid middle class background. When Bennett left school he worked initially with his father's firm and then in 1889 he obtained a position with a London firm of solicitors. During these employments he had written short articles for various newspapers and eventually in 1898 his first novel *A Man from the North* was published and this marked the end of his legal career. He married Marguerite Soulié in 1907 while living in Paris and the marriage lasted until late into 1920. In the meantime he had successfully developed his career as a writer.

In 1922 Bennett acquired the lease of 75 Cadogan Square which he felt 'rather noble in the way of houses'.[3] His study looked out at the back on to a mulberry tree and the house was shared with his secretary who lived with her mother on the top floor and a staff which comprised a valet, cook and various maids. Unlike Lord Stockton's acacia tree, Arnold

Bennett's mulberry tree remains in good health.

The atmosphere of Cadogan Square appears to have been beneficial, for Bennett, having experienced something akin to writer's block at the beginning of the Twenties, in the autumn of 1923 published a novel called *Riceyman Steps* which re-established him and was regarded by some as a masterpiece. At about the same time as he moved into Cadogan Square, Bennett had met Dorothy Cheston, an architect's daughter intent upon making a career on the stage, and she became a frequent visitor to Bennett's new home. It was in his study one evening that he declared his love and in 1926 she bore him a daughter. Marriage was impossible as Bennett's wife, a Catholic, would not divorce him. Bennett's income peaked in 1927 when he earned £22.000. From then on, however, financial difficulties gathered momentum and in 1929 he was finding the house in Cadogan Square not only costly but difficult to run as Dorothy, now in residence, was not used to managing domestic staff. On top of these complications, the lease was coming to an end and Bennett refused to pay the higher rent which was now being sought. He completed work on *Imperial Palace* in October 1930 and the following month he left Cadogan Square for Chiltern Court in Baker Street where he died on 27 March 1931 in his sixty-fourth year.

And so with Arnold Bennett the story thus far ends. It will continue for another writer to record at another time. The Cadogan Estate has done and continues to do much to improve and to maintain the fair face of Chelsea while the Cadogan family has contributed greatly in the sphere of public service. May both continue to prosper.

Family Trees

Ancient Cadogan Family Line

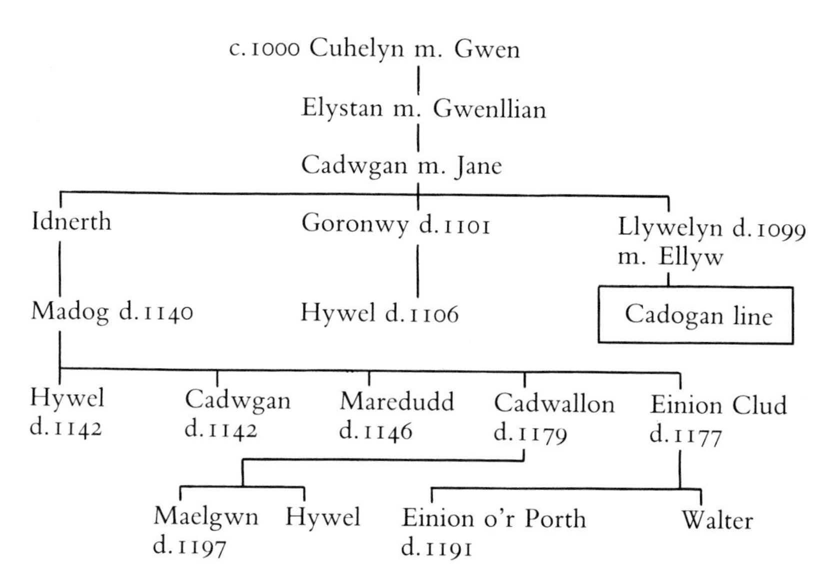

Family Trees

Modern Cadogan Family Line – Abridged

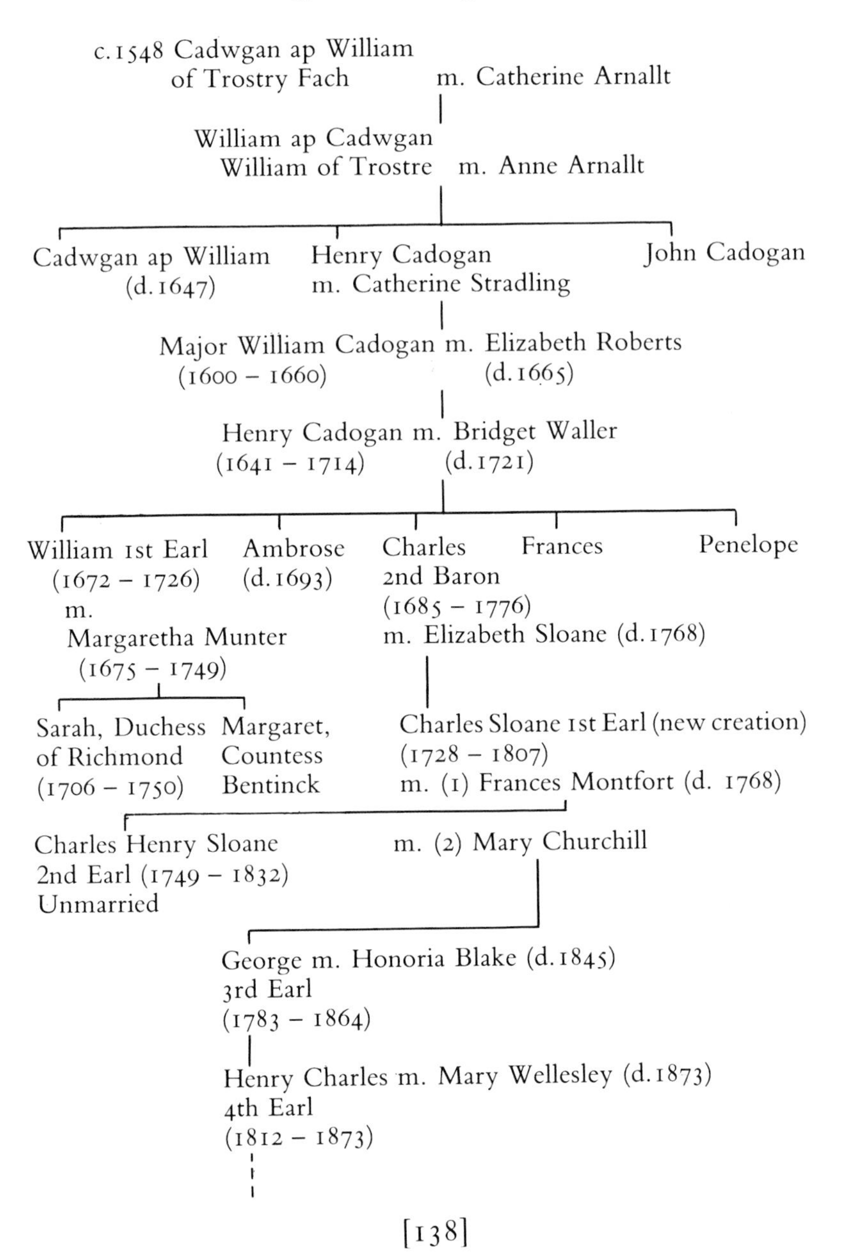

George Henry m. (1) Lady Beatrix Craven (d. 1907)
5th Earl m. (2) Adele Palagio (No issue)
(1840 – 1915)

Gerald Oakley m. Lilian Coxon
6th Earl
(1869 – 1933)

William Gerald Charles m. (1) Primrose Yarde-Buller
7th Earl m. (2) Cecilia Hamilton–Wedderburn (No issue)
(1914 –)

Charles Gerald John m. Lady Phillipa Dorothy Bluett Wallop (d. 1984)
Viscount Chelsea
(1937 –)

Edward Charles
(1966 –)

Sloane Family Line – Extract

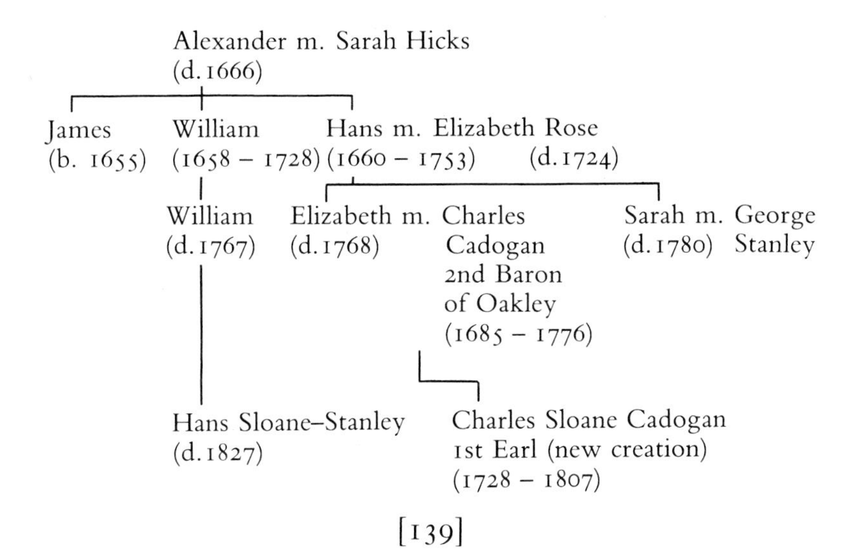

APPENDIX I

Elizabeth Cadogan (d. 1665) – Last Will & Testament

IN THE NAME OF GOD AMEN.

I Elizabeth Cadogan of the City of Dublin widow (the Relict of William Cadogan late of Ardbraccan in the County of Eastmeath Esquire deceased) being broke in body but of sound and perfect memory praised be God do make this my last Will and Testament in manner and form following.

Firstly I bequeath my Soul unto God my Creator and Redeemer and my body to be interred in a decent and orderly manner in Christchurch Dublin by my deceased husband and my Daughter Ann Waddington.

Item my Will is and I do hereby devise unto my Servant Mary Lee one store of Ewes.

Item I do devise and bequeath unto my Servant Jane Price one store of Ewes two heifers of two years old one English Cow and five pounds in money.

Item I will and bequeath unto my Servant Anne Cartman two young heifers of two years old and one Cow.

Item I bequeath unto my Servant Mire Priall the bed and bed clothes which she has and usually layeth on in Dublin one English Cow and twenty Ewes.

Item I devise unto Elizabeth Stuart two heifers of Age last year.

Item I devise and bequeath unto my nephew John Salisbury two breeding mares the one bay and the other black Six English Cows and three store Ewes.

Item I devise unto John Barnes the younger one breeding mare.

Item I devise unto Sir Jerome Alexander Baronet Five pounds and unto his Lady Five pounds to buy them Rings, and four pounds unto their Daughter Miss Elizabeth Alexander to buy her a piece of plate.

Item I devise unto the widow Elliott of Dublin the Relict of one Michael Elliott twenty shillings yearly during her life issuing both out of Inheritance and Chattles Real and unto Thomasin Hill of Galway Five Pounds.

Item I devise unto Sir Henry Waddington Knight Five pounds unto my Cousin John Santhey Esquire Five pounds unto William Hancocke Esquire Five pounds and unto Symon Creme Five pounds in reference to a trust reposed in them mentioned in a Deed indented Dated the twenty eighth day of December instant and also to my dear Cousin Mrs Frances Santhey Wife of the said John Santhey Five pounds to buy her a Ring to wear in memory of me.

Item My Will is and I do hereby devise and bequeath unto my dearly beloved Son Mr Henry Cadogan his heirs Executors Administrators and Assigns respectively all my Lands tenements and hereditaments and all my goods and Chattels both Real and Personal except such monies plate jewells apparel and goods which by Deed Indented dated the twenty eighth of December instant made betwixt me of the one part and the said Sir Henry Waddington John Santhey William Hancocke Symon Creme and Henry Cadogan of the other part, have been before the day of the Date hereof given granted or disposed of. It being not my Intent by this my last Will to release Abridge or annul the said Deeds Rents Debts Dues and demands whatsoever (except before excepted) whereof I the said Elizabeth Cadogan am either seized or possessed or have or ought to have enjoy be seized or possessed of either in my name or in the right of my said Late husband William Cadogan Esquire Deceased And of this my last Will and Testament I the said Elizabeth Cadogan Do make constitute and appoint my said Son Henry Cadogan my only and

Sole Executor.

In Witness whereof I the said Elizabeth Cadogan Give and Do publish this my last Will and Testament in writing under my hand and Seal this twenty ninth day of December in the year of Our Lord One Thousand six hundred sixty four.

Elizabeth Cadogan

Signed sealed and published in the presence of

Thomas Bladen
Walter Nugent
Henry Salisbury
John Santhey

The 1st Earl Cadogan (1672–1726) Last Will & Testament

In the Name of God Amen – I William Earl Cadogan do hereby revoke annul and make void all former Wills by me at any time heretofore made and do make this my last Will and Testament that is to say I do ratify and confirm the articles of agreement I executed with the late Duke of Richmond upon the marriage of his son and my daughter the now Duke and Duchess of Richmond and I do also ratify and confirm the settlement I made upon my brother Colonel Charles Cadogan at the time of his marriage.

Item my mind and will is that if my said son and Daughter the Duke and Duchess of Richmond shall claim demand and recover any part of my Estate in Holland by reason of any of the Laws or Customs there that the same shall be made good and reimbursed to my Estate in Holland out of the monies and Estate I agreed to pay and settle on the marriage of my said son and Daughter Richmond and I do give to my youngest Daughter the Lady Margaret Cadogan and her Children all such monies which shall be so reimbursed and for want of Issue of my said youngest Daughter I give the same to my said brother his heirs and Executors.

Item my mind and Will is that whatever Estate I have or am entitled unto after the several deceases of my said son and Daughter the Duke and Duchess of Richmond without Issue of their bodies by or virtue of the said Marriage articles I do give devise and bequeath the same to my said youngest Daughter and her Issue and for want of such Issue to my said Brother his heirs and Executors.

Item I do give and bequeath unto my five Nieces Daughters of my sister Dame Penelope Prendergast one thousand pounds a piece to be paid out of the Debt which my Nephew Sir Thomas Prendergast Baronet owes me and the remainder of the said Debt I give and release to him he ratifying and making good to his Mother her Joynture and paying all sums of money he now owes and shall owe her.

Item I give to my said youngest Daughter Margaret the sum of eight thousand pounds out of my Estate in Holland and I give to my Wife during her life the enjoyment of the remainder of all my real and personal Estate in Holland not herein before disposed of and then I give the same to my said youngest Daughter and her Children and in default of such Issue then to my said Daughter the Duchess of Richmond and her Children and in default of Issue then to my said brother and in default of his Issue then to the said Sir Thomas Prendergast his heirs and Executors.

Item I give to my said Sister the Lady Prendergast and her Executors my house in Jermyn Street and also my House in Piccadilly now let to Mr Dearing and also the sum of one thousand five hundred pounds of lawful money of Great Britain.

Item I will that my Executors hereinafter named shall lay out fifty pounds to buy a Communion plate for the use of the Church of Caversham in Oxfordshire.

Item I give all my family pictures to the said Duke of Richmond.

Item I do give devise and bequeath unto the Right Honourable the Earl of Shelburn the Lord Carteret and my said Brother Colonel Cadogan their heirs and Executors and administrators all my Manors Houses Lands Tenements and hereditaments with their and every of their appurtenances in England and also my plate Jewels household Goods and personal Estate whatsoever not herein before disposed of in trust that they shall sell and dispose of the same and by and out of the monies to be raised by such sale or sales pay and satisfy in the first place all such sums of money as I am engaged or have agreed or Covenanted to pay by virtue of the said articles executed by me upon the said Marriage of my said son and Daughter Richmond and then to pay and satisfy all other my Just debts and funeral Charges and out of the residue and overplus the rest I do give to my said youngest Daughter the sum of twelve thousand pounds and the remainder thereof shall be vested in Lands to the use of my said youngest Daughter and the heirs of her body and for want of such Issue to my said Brother and his heirs and I do appoint my Executors hereafter named to be likewise trustees for securing and laying out the sum of money agreed by the said articles made on the marriage of the said Duke and Duchess of Richmond to be paid by me according to the true intent and meaning of the said articles and I desire that the said Duke of Richmond may have the preference in the purchase of any part of my said real and personal Estate devised to be sold as aforesaid and I desire my Entry Coach in Holland may be sold and the monies arising thereby may be paid to my said Executors upon the trusts herein before mentioned.

Item I do give and devise to my Servant Francis Bland who has attended upon me in my present Illness the annual sum of forty pounds to be paid him quarterly at the four usual Feasts or days of payment in the year during his life without any deduction or abatement whatsoever the first payment to be made at such of the said Feasts as shall next happen after my decease and I also give him the sum of one hundred pounds and I give to each of my menial Servants Six months of their yearly Wages over and above what shall be due to them respectively at my decease and I lastly do make and constitute the said Lord Shelburn Lord Carteret and brother Cadogan Executors of this my last Will and Testament upon the trusts herein before mentioned and desire to be buried with all the privacy imaginable and not above one hundred and fifty pounds be expended in and about my funeral. In witness whereof I here unto set my hand and seal this twenty seventh day of June in the twelfth year of the Reign of his present Majesty King George anno Dom One thousand seven hundred and twenty six. *Cadogan.*

Signed sealed and published by the said Earl Cadogan in our presence who have in his presence attested the same and subscribed our names

J Hancok
Cornet Charles Sanderson

Notes and References

CHAPTER I

1 Walter Gropius (1883–1969). Leading German architect of the Modern Movement and teacher who designed 66 Old Church Street in 1936.

Henry Holland (1745–1806). Architect whose principal work was the alteration and enlargement of Carlton House, Pall Mall, as a residence for the Prince of Wales in 1788. A few of Holland's 'Hans Town' houses remain, including 123 and 139 Sloane Street and, possibly, 30 and 34 Hans Place.

R. Norman Shaw. Victorian architect whose works included Cragside, Northumberland 1869–84, Scotland Yard 1889–90, the Gaiety Theatre, Aldwych 1903 and the Piccadilly Hotel 1905–08. During the period 1879–82 he designed 68 and 72 Cadogan Place.

2 See Chapter XIV.

3 Jane Austen (1775–1817) the novelist is reputed to have stayed at 23 Hans Place while Percy Bysshe Shelley (1792–1822) the poet is noted as having passed a few days at the home of Letitia Elizabeth Landen, also a novelist and poet, at 25 Hans Place. Both houses were completely rebuilt in the 1870s.

4 *Daily Mail*, 17 September 1985, p.17.

CHAPTER III

1 From the letters and papers of William Cadogan – MS.2541 *Ormonde Papers 1640–49*. National Library of Ireland.

2 *Calendar of State Papers – Ireland*. PRO, London. SP Dom.Int.I 92.

3 An Irish acre is 7840 square yards. An English acre is 4840 square yards.

4 Transcription of will in Appendix I.

5 Transcription of will in Appendix II.

CHAPTER IV

1 DNB and Richard Cannon's *Historical Record 5th Dragoon Guards* p.28, 1839.

2 3 Geo. II 1730 Cap.8.

3 Lease in the County Library, Royal County of Berkshire, D/EX. 258/12.

4 Original correspondence held at the British Library.
5 *Vitruvius Britannicus* by C. Campbell c.1717.
6 *Marlborough His Life and Times* by W.S. Churchill, 1938, p.642.
7 *The House of Commons 1715–1754* Volume I p.513 History of Parliament Trust.

CHAPTER V

1 Conveyance of Beaufort House dated 25 July 1737 from the Duke of Beaufort to Sir Hans Sloane. GLC Record Office (Old Middlesex Registry Book 2 No.585).

CHAPTER VI

1 *A Concise Law Dictionary* by P.G. Osbourne 1964.

CHAPTER VII

1 *Remarks and Collections* Volume VI, January 1717 – May 1719 by Thomas Hearne, 1902.
2 Guidebook published in 1761 quoted in an unpublished manuscript by G.L-W. MacKenzie 'Twelve Lordships since the Conquest: Caversham Park a Retrospect', Berkshire County Library.
3 *Diaries of Mrs Lybbe Powys* ed E.J. Climenson 1899 quoted in *Capability Brown* by Dorothy Stroud 1975.
4 *The Letters and Journals of Lady Mary Coke* Volume 2 quoted in G.L-W. Mackenzie *op.cit.*
5 Ibid.
6 *Memoirs of the Reign of George III* by Horace Walpole, quoted in G.L-W. Mackenzie *op.cit.*
7 *Biographical Index to the House of Lords*, 1808.
8 A Private Act of Parliament to dissolve the marriage between the 1st Earl Cadogan (New Creation) and Mary Churchill 37 Geo.III No.116.
9 *The Buildings of England: London – Cities of London and Westminster* by Sir Nikolaus Pevsner, p.539. *Survey of London* Volume XIII Part II 'St Margarets'. LCC.

CHAPTER VIII

1 53 Geo. III Cap. 190.
2 6 Geo.IV Cap. 16
3 6 Geo. IV Cap.17.
4 *History and Description of Chelsea* by Thomas Faulkner 1829.

Notes and References

CHAPTER IX

1 *History and Description of Chelsea* by Thomas Faulkner 1829 p.229.
2 Ibid. p.231
3 *A History of the Peninsular War* by Sir Charles Oman, 1902 edn. Vol VI p.401 quoting diary of William Gavin.
4 *Wellington – The Years of the Sword* by Elizabeth Longford 1969.
5 *Naval and Military Gazette*, obituary, 17 September 1864. p.595.
6 Marshall's *Royal Naval Biography* 1827 p.197.
7 *Memoirs of Gerald Blunt of Chelsea* edited by Reginald Blunt 1911 p.104
8 Sir Nikolaus Pevsner p.629 *op.cit.*
9 *Memoirs of Gerald Blunt* p.115.

CHAPTER X

1 *West London Press* 3 July 1896.
2 *The World* 18 June 1912 p.926.
3 *Before the Deluge* by The Hon. Sir Edward Cadogan pp.11, 12 1961.
4 *The World* 18 June 1912 p. 926.
5 *Blenheim Revisited* by Hugh Montgomery-Massingberd 1985.
6 *The World* 18 June 1912.

CHAPTER XI

1 *Evening News* magazine 20 June 1980.
2 *The Building News* 24 September 1858 p.952.
3 *The Builder* 19 January 1889 p.50.

CHAPTER XII

1 *Survey of London – Grosvenor Estate* LCC pp.41, 42.
2 Ibid. p.47.

CHAPTER XIII

1 *Country Life* 20 February 1932 pp.212, 213.
2 *West London Press* 26 January 1962.

CHAPTER XIV

1 *Interbuild* December 1960 pp.15–18.
2 *Winds of Change 1914–1939* Harold Macmillan 1966 pp.30, 33.
3 *Writer By Trade – A View of Arnold Bennett* by Dudley Barker. 1966.

A Select Bibliography

Barker D. *Writer by Trade – A View of Arnold Bennett*, George Allen & Unwin 1966.

Bartrum P.C. *Welsh Genealogies* A.D. 390 – 1400, University of Wales Press 1974.

Bartrum P.C. *Welsh Genealogies* A.D. 1400 – 1500, The National Library of Wales 1983.

Beaver A. *Memorials of Old Chelsea*, SR Publishers 1971.

Bottigheimer K. *The Adventurers in the Cromwellian Settlement of Ireland*, Oxford at the Clarendon Press 1971.

Bradney Sir J. *A History of Monmouthshire*, London 1923.

Brooks E.St.J. *Sir Hans Sloane*, The Batchworth Press 1954.

Brough J. *The Prince and The Lily*, Hodder & Stoughton 1975.

Cadogan Sir E. *Before the Deluge*, John Murray 1961.

Churchill W.S. *Marlborough His Life and Times*, Harrap 1934.

Davison B.K. *Castles*, Frederick Warne 1979.

de Beer G.T. *Sir Hans Sloane and The British Museum*, Oxford University Press 1953.

Faulkner T. *History and Description of Chelsea* 1829.

Firth C. *Cromwell's Army*, Methuen 1962.

Green D. *Sarah Duchess of Marlborough*, Collins 1967.

Holme T. *Chelsea*, Hamish Hamilton 1972.

Kroyer P. *The Story of Lindsey House, Chelsea*, Country Life 1956.

Langtry L. *Days I Knew*, Hutchinson.

Lloyd J.E. *A History of Wales*, Longmans 1912.

Macmillan H. *Winds of Change* 1914–1939, Macmillan 1966.

Moody T.W. and others *A New History of Ireland*, Oxford at the Clarendon Press 1976.

Palmer A.N. *Country Townships of Wrexham.*

Pevsner, Sir N. *The Buildings of England*, Penguin Books 1954–66.

Prendergast J. *The Cromwellian Settlement of Ireland*, Longman 1865.

Rudé G. *Hanoverian London* 1714–1808, Secker & Warburg 1971.

Sloane W.R. *Sir Hans Sloane – Legend and Lineage*, Privately published 1981.

Smith P. *Houses of the Welsh Countryside*, HMSO 1975.

Storey G. *People and Places – An East Anglian Miscellany*, Terence Dalton 1973.

Stroud D. *Capability Brown*, Faber & Faber 1975.

Stroud D. *Henry Holland*, Art & Technics 1950.
Thompson F.M.L. *English Landed Society in the Nineteenth Century*, Routledge & Kegan Paul 1963.
Young P. *Oliver Cromwell*, Severn House 1975.
Articles
Country Life 'Lord Cadogan's Sheep (Culford)' 10 Feb 1906.
Country Life 'Cadogan Square' by Mark Girouard, 16 & 23 November 1978.

AUTHORITIES CONSULTED

England: Bath Reference Library; British Library; Buckinghamshire County Council Record Office; Chelsea Library Local Studies Department; Chelsea Society Annual Reports; Cheshire County Council Record Office; City of Westminster Archives Department; Devon County Council Record Office; Durham County Council Record Office; Goodwood Estate Co Ltd; GLC Historic Buildings Department; HM Tower of London; House of Commons Public Information Office; House of Lords Record Office; Isle of Wight Record Office; National Army Museum Library; Naval Historical Library MOD; Norfolk County Council Record Office; Oxfordshire County Council Record Office; Public Record Office, London; Royal County of Berkshire Library; Royal Institute of British Architects Library; Royal Institution of Chartered Surveyors Library; Shropshire County Council Record Office; Suffolk County Council Record Office; Wellcome Institute for the History of Medicine; Westminster Abbey Library; Westminster School; West Sussex Record Office.

Holland: Netherlands National Archives The Hague; Royal Archives The Hague.

Northern Ireland: Public Record Office of Northern Ireland; Ulster Historical Foundation.

Republic of Ireland: Christ Church Cathedral Dublin; Genealogical Office Dublin Castle; Irish Manuscripts Commission; Meath County Library; National Library of Ireland; Public Record Office of Ireland; Registry of Deeds; Trinity College Library University of Dublin; Westmeath County Library.

Wales: Clwyd County Council Record Office; Dyfed County Council Record Office; Gwent County Council Record Office; Gwynedd County Council Record Office; Powys County Council Record Office; Royal Commission on Ancient and Historical Monuments of Wales; The National Library of Wales.

Illustration Acknowledgements

Chelsea Street Plan (Chapter 1), Geographers A–Z Map Co Ltd, based on the Ordnance Survey map with the permission of the Controller of Her Majesty's Stationery Office, Crown copyright reserved; 1st Earl Cadogan, the National Army Museum; Sarah Cadogan and her husband the Duke of Richmond, the Trustees of the Goodwood Collections; Sir Hans Sloane, the National Portrait Gallery; Hamilton's Map of Chelsea, the Royal Borough of Kensington and Chelsea; Mrs Frances Cadogan, the Paul Mellon Centre for Studies in British Art; 1st Earl Cadogan of the New Creation and 2nd Earl, Paul Mellon Centre; The Pavilion, The British Library (K Top xxxviii 4 dd 617); Henry Holland, the British Architectural Library/RIBA; 9 Cheyne Walk, Brian Evans; 66 Old Church Street, Friend & Falcke; Harold Macmillan, the Macmillan Family Archive; Arnold Bennett, National Portrait Gallery; Lillie Langtry, Société Jersiaise, Jersey Museum, C.I.

The following drawings and maps were prepared by J.W. Pearman: the Cadogan Estate today, Lower Trostre Farmhouse today, The Manor House, Oakley, The Manor of Chelsea in 1753, 33 Grosvenor Street.

Index

Numbers in italic refer to pages on which illustrations will be found.

Index

Index

Index